The public theology think tank

C000133412

what Theos is

Theos is a public theology think tank which exists to undertake research and provide commentary on social and political arrangements. The word "Theos" and our descriptor, "the public theology think tank", reflect our overall aim of putting God "back" into the public domain. Theos is about social, public theology; about public wisdom.

what Theos stands for

Faith is on the public agenda in a way that is unprecedented in recent times. Theos aims to shape events, not simply react to them. We aspire to speak wisdom into the increasingly crowded market-place of ideas and seek to demonstrate that religion in public debate is not dangerous or plain irrelevant, but that it is crucial to enable such public debate to connect with the communities it seeks to serve. We believe that faith is personal but it can never be private.

what Theos works on

Theos undertakes research on a wide range of subject areas. We believe that every issue is a moral issue and reject notions of a sacred/secular divide.

what Theos provides

Theos provides:

- high-quality research, reports and publications;
- an events' programme (including public debates, an annual Theos lecture and an extensive fringe programme at the party conferences);
- news, information and analysis to media companies and other opinion formers, with a one-stop information line available to journalists; and
- an informative website, www.theosthinktank.co.uk

In addition to our independently driven work, Theos provides research, analysis and advice to individuals and organisations across the private, public and not-for-profit sectors. Our unique position within the think tank sector means that we have the capacity to develop proposals that carry values - with an eye to demonstrating what really works. Our staff and consultants have strong public affairs experience, an excellent research track record and a high level of theological literacy. We are practised in campaigning, media relations, detailed policy development and effecting policy change.

Published by Theos in 2006
© Theos

ISBN: 0 9554453 0 2
ISBN-13: 978 0 9554453 0 9

For further information and subscription details please contact:

Theos
Licence Department
34 Buckingham Palace Road
London
SW1W 0RE
United Kingdom

T 020 7828 7777
E hello@theosthinktank.co.uk
www.theosthinktank.co.uk

"Doing God"

A Future for Faith in the Public Square

by Nick Spencer

acknowledgements

The author alone is responsible for the success or failure of the arguments in this report, but he would like to acknowledge the contribution that a number of other people have made and to thank them sincerely for it.

Paul Bickley was an excellent research assistant and provided a rich source of valuable information. David Landrum offered characteristically intelligent and provocative comments on an earlier draft. Danny Kruger, Lucy Winkett and David Ashford all read the manuscript and gave me thoughtful and helpful advice. Margaret Reece and Jeremy Sweetland gave invaluable assistance in proofing and editing the final draft.

My greatest thanks are due to Paul Woolley who did me an honour in asking me to write this inaugural report, provided valuable editorial advice throughout and steered the document through from conception to publication.

Nick Spencer
September 2006

foreword

At first I experienced moments of perplexity and arrest of life, and though I did not know what to do or how to live; and I felt lost and became dejected. But this passed and I went on living as before. Then these moments of perplexity began to recur oftener and oftener, and always in the same form. They were always expressed by the questions: What is it for? What does it lead to?

Leo Tolstoy, *A Confession*

Tolstoy wrote of the educated elite of his day that the faith of the majority could be summarised in the word "progress". For a while, he had accepted the conventional wisdom of nineteenth century Russia that religion was impossible for a serious, educated person, and had no place in public life. But, as he records in his *Confession*, he could not escape those occasions when he was aware of the lack of wholeness in his world-view and the lack of resources to confront the most important questions in his life.

Our society is experiencing a similar "moment of perplexity". Issues of belief and faith, of how human beings perceive the world, have rarely been so important in society, or so badly misunderstood. In international affairs, in education, in the most pressing debates in medical ethics, the modern mind may identify with the words, "I felt that what I had been standing on had collapsed and that I had nothing left under my feet. What I had lived on no longer existed, and there was nothing left."

As a society, we must decide how we will respond to this moment of collective confusion - can we seek to go on living as before? Or, like Tolstoy, will we reassess the importance of faith to individuals and society. By increasing public understanding of faith and its contribution to public life, *"Doing God": A Future for Faith in the Public Square* aims to encourage such reassessment.

The first part of the report considers why it is simply not possible to take faith out of the public arena. Dealing as it does with questions of identity, existence and environment, faith will not allow itself to be treated in this way. But the report also considers the benefits that faith has given society as a whole. It argues that the secular public square, properly understood, is a Christian legacy and one that requires an ongoing Christian presence in order to remain true to itself.

The second part of the report examines reasons why faith will play an increasingly significant role in public life. It goes beyond the obvious - such as the rise of radical Islam - and identifies three trends: the return of civil society, the pursuit of happiness and the politics of identity.

Many secularist commentators argue that the growing role of faith in society represents a dangerous development. However, they fail to recognise that public atheism is itself an intolerant faith position. If we pay attention to what is actually happening in the United Kingdom and beyond, we will see that religiously - inspired public engagement need not be sectarian and can, in fact, be radically inclusive. This report argues that faith is not just important for human flourishing and the renewal of society but that society can only flourish if faith is given space to makes its contribution and its challenge.

Together, we welcome the publication of this report and look forward to the contribution that Theos will make to future debates.

The Most Revd Dr Rowan Williams
The Archbishop of Canterbury

Cardinal Cormac Murphy-O'Connor
The Archbishop of Westminster

November 2006

introduction -
a God-flavoured fudge

Tony Blair's interview with Michael Parkinson in March 2006 was revelatory, although not in the way many people thought.

Talking about his decision to go to war in Iraq, Blair said:

> In the end there is a judgement that, well, I think if you have faith about these things then you realise that judgement is made by other people, and also by…

He didn't get the chance to finish his sentence. The veteran interviewer pounced on the scoop. "What do you mean by that?" The Prime Minister's response was faltering but clear:

> I mean by other people, by, if you believe in God, it's made by God as well and that judgement in the end has to be, you know, you do your … When you're faced with a decision like that, and some of those decisions have been very, very difficult, as I say, most of all because you know there are people's lives, not just, this isn't a matter of a policy here or a thing there but their lives, and in some case, their death … The only way you can take a decision like that is to try to do the right thing according to your conscience, and for the rest of it you leave it, as I say, to the judgement that history will make.[1]

The word "God" had been uttered and, worse still, in the context of war. The media response was instant and astounded.

The interview, which had been trailed as the lead item on most news programmes on most networks the previous evening, claimed the front page. Was Blair claiming God told him to invade Iraq? Was he insinuating God approved of his decision? Was he suggesting that prayer had strengthened his resolve to go to war? Was he finding a way of avoiding public censure?

The answer was no, in each case. He was saying, albeit very hesitantly, that he believed he would one day be judged by God for his decision to go to war; not, one would have thought, a particularly unusual thought for a Christian. After all, "Christian believes he will be judged by God" is not, in the usual run of things, headline material.

If the interview revealed little about Tony Blair - we already knew he was a Christian and presumably, therefore, that he believed in ultimate moral judgement by his creator - it revealed rather more about the public, and its extreme nervousness about any hint of the divine in public discourse. "The British people have long appeared cautious, if not downright suspicious, of politicians who claim to be motivated by faith," the BBC told us.[2] Mr Blair's comments were "bizarre", remarked Dr Evan Harris, a Liberal Democrat MP and honorary associate of the National Secular Society, who went on to warn politicians against making "references to deity" in public life.[3]

The Archbishop of Canterbury, Rowan Williams, was more sympathetic in an interview with the *Guardian* newspaper a few weeks later. Blair's interview revealed, "how very difficult it is for us … culturally … to understand what people mean by talking about the judgement of God." Ultimately the Prime Minister was:

> trying to say something which I hope any religious believer would say, which is when I make a decision, particularly a really appallingly difficult decision, I know that finally what makes right or wrong is not what I think or even what the general public thinks, but God.[4]

A few weeks later the Prime Minister was speaking at a conference held at RUACH Ministries, a Christian Pentecostal church in Brixton. In the Q&A after his talk (on political engagement) he was asked why he didn't speak about God more in public.[5]

"Look what happens when I do," he replied.

God, it seems, does not belong in the public square.

"extreme religious views"

Is Tony Blair an exception? Does his widely-known Christian faith mark him out for special scrutiny? Or was the Parkinson furore more about the uniquely sensitive case of the Iraq war than about any alleged British unease with the holy?

The annual rash of "winterval" and "political correctness gone mad" stories suggest not. Every year some local council renames Christmas in order, allegedly, not to give offence to other faiths. Last year, Lambeth Council renamed its Christmas lights "Winter lights", although a council spokeswoman subsequently claimed it was a junior-level decision that happened to go into print by accident.[6] Torbay Council insisted on removing a cross from the wall of a crematorium chapel for fear of upsetting other faiths.[7]

And it's not just local councils. The Welsh Assembly recently stopped public funding of "Teen Challenge" on the basis that its successful drug rehabilitation programme included spiritual elements considered to fall within the category of "proselytism".[8] A church-run shelter for the homeless in Kings Lynn was warned that its funding would be cut off if it continued to say grace before meals, made Bibles publicly available and refused to remove mention of Christianity from its legal objectives.[9] Various Christian Unions have been put under pressure to admit non-Christians onto their board. Edinburgh University was considering banning Bibles from its student halls of residence on the basis that they are "discriminatory" and make students of other faiths feel unwelcome.[10]

One Norman Clark captured these sentiments well in a letter to the *Independent* in May 2006 concerning "the continued presence of Ruth Kelly in the Government".

> Here we have a woman of extreme religious views consecutively in charge of departments where her personal views must be in direct conflict with the requirements of her offices. If she claims this is not the case then surely she must be a huge hypocrite. Democratic government should not be about having extremists of any description in power.

In this way local councils and *Independent* readers make windows into men's souls and, not liking what they find there, close their cheque books or recommend the job centre. God, it appears, is being slowly and purposefully evicted from the public square, just as he was from the preamble to the EU constitution.

the return of faith

Except, of course, he isn't.

Only the wilfully blind or those with a well-developed martyr complex could think that twenty-first century Britain was actively hostile to religious belief or that God has been elbowed out of the public square. Not only is "faith" back in the public square, but it is somewhere near the centre.

This is partly due to its inherently controversial nature, controversy acting like a floatation device in TV running orders. The government's determination to push through an expansion of state-funded voluntary-aided faith schools and its eagerness to work with faith organisations in setting up its city academies has brought God firmly into the public square, and with him the rather tired (non-) question about whether he made the world 4,000 or 4,000 million years BC.

The tension between diversity and cohesion that pervades modern British society was put under the spotlight when a Muslim schoolgirl from Luton took her school to court for the right to wear clothes that reflected a stricter version of modesty than her (already modest) school uniform offered. God, albeit himself in a different uniform, was again lurking in the background.[11]

Jerry Springer, Behzti and provocative cartoons all had a similar effect. Ian Mayes, reader's editor for the *Guardian*, responding to several readers who wrote to him asking/complaining about that paper's increased coverage of religion, wrote:

> There is undoubtedly more discussion of religion in the pages of the paper but that reflects its increasing importance in politics ... A crude measure is the number of stories in the *Guardian* that mention the word Christian: in 1985, 770; in 1995, 1,221; and in 2005, 2,341. A search for the word Muslim showed: 1985, 408; 1995, 1,106; and in 2005, 2,114.[12]

God's presence in the public square hasn't necessarily been linked to controversy, however. The Faith Communities' Capacity Building Fund and the Faith Based Regeneration Network are hardly household names, but each has grown significantly in size and importance over recent years. As the philosopher, Julian Baggini, has rightly observed:

> When the UK Prime Minister's spokesperson remarked in 2003 that "We don't do God" what was striking was that until that point it went without saying that politicians don't overtly discuss religion. The need to rule god-talk out was a symptom that it was coming back in.[13]

In reality, this shift in British culture seems to be little more than an (albeit rather pale) reflection of broader global culture.

Shortly after Tony Blair's appearance on the Parkinson show, Radio 3 devoted an entire week of its programme '*Night Waves*' to "The Return of Faith", "exploring the resurgence of religion across the globe".[14] The debate about the preamble to the EU constitution rather obscured the fact that the Constitution laid on the Commission the duty to have a regular, structured and transparent dialogue with the churches.

As Richard Chartres, Bishop of London, has said:

> From the point of view of somebody who is interested in the contribution which faith communities have to make to the contemporary Europe, the Constitution actually represents a bit of an advance on where we've been up to now.

More broadly still, a study of the non/separation of religion and state round the world in the twenty-first century, published in *Comparative Political Studies* in June 2006, observed that:

> more than a century since the founders of the social sciences began to predict the demise of religion in modern times, SRAS (separation of religion and state) is the exception and GIR (government involvement in religion) is the norm.[15]

the assumption that we live in a secularised world is false: The world today, with some exceptions … is as furiously religious as it ever was, and in some places more so than ever.

The author, Jonathan Fox, elaborated on this in several ways. Between 1990 and 2002 there had been a slight *increase* in government involvement in religion worldwide. By 2002, government involvement in religion was "the norm" and separation of religion and state "the exception". And contrary to the predictions and indeed received wisdom, current data show that modernisation is associated with *higher* rather than lower levels of government involvement in religion. He concluded:

> The findings here challenge basic assumptions made by major elements of social science and political science theory. They are sufficiently unequivocal and strong to warrant a major reconsideration of our assumptions regarding the role of religion in modern times in general and the role of religion in democracies in particular.

The traditional theory of secularisation, developed by such luminaries as Auguste Comte, Herbert Spencer, Emile Durkheim, Max Weber, Karl Marx and Sigmund Freud, which reached its hubristic apogee in the 1960s was, if not quite in tatters, then certainly looking threadbare.

The sociologist, Peter Berger, who wrote in *The New York Times* in 1968, "[By] the twenty-first century, religious believers are likely to be found only in small sects, huddled together to resist a worldwide secular culture", wrote in his book, *The Desecularisation of the World,* in 1999:

> the assumption that we live in a secularised world is false: The world today, with some exceptions … is as furiously religious as it ever was, and in some places more so than ever.[16]

God was back, not just in the UK but pretty much everywhere. Not uncontroversially of course. But then God could never claim to be an uncontroversial figure.

a God-flavoured fudge

So where does all this leave us in the UK and what will it mean for us in the twenty-first century? The answer is that most characteristically English of things: a fudge wrapped in a muddle inside an uncertainty.

By comparison, at least those happy individuals in France and the United States know where they stand. The US remains, according to Jonathan Fox, the *only* country in the world with full separation of religion and state. France has its well-established and fiercely protected culture of *laïcité*. Neither country is exactly free from religious controversy (to put it mildly) but both know, at least in theory, where the line is drawn.

Up until recently there had, at least, been something of an ad hoc resolution in Britain. The role of religion in public life was widely thought to have been satisfactorily settled, in practice, if not in theory. There was, as Sunder Katwala, Director of the Fabian Society, has written, a:

> largely absent-minded maintenance of an established Church, whose leaders' public moderation often bordered on agnosticism within a society which thought of itself as increasingly secular.[17]

That arrangement was itself relatively harmless. Indeed, when considered alongside the various remaining ceremonial and cultural links between church and state, it was possibly even positive, at least for reasons of social cohesion and tourism. There may have been a few mopping up exercises remaining - bishops in the Lords, blasphemy laws, perhaps even disestablishment - but these were little more than the finishing touches to a newly deconsecrated public square.

Now that the secularisation theory is looking so weak and God isn't quite as dead as previous generations had thought, we are not sure what to do.

This report argues that, whilst there is no reason to suggest that this characteristic British fudge will go away, it will become increasingly God-flavoured. Having been evicted from the public square through one exit, God has not only appeared at another, but looks as if he's making himself comfortable. Whether we like it or not, and this report acknowledges the fact that some do not, we will be "doing God" in the future.

It hopes to explain why in two parts. The first, which encompasses chapters 1 and 2, addresses the traditional arguments against "doing God", and argues that, for various reasons, they are deficient. It recognises, however, that a number of these reasons contain important points and that anyone who wishes to mix God and Caesar must acknowledge and address them if they wish to be taken seriously.

The second part shifts from the defensive to look at the positive reasons why we in twenty-first century Britain will be "doing God" rather more than we did in the twentieth century. It goes beyond the obvious and widely reported trends - the growing Muslim population, the emergence of political Islam, the peculiar persistence of Christian self-identification, the appearance of vociferous minority religious groups - to examine three reasons in particular.

Chapter 3 argues that the melancholy, long, withdrawing roar of state welfare provision is exposing a long-hidden shore of civil society, in which religious groups in general and the churches in particular have and are playing a significant role. This alone is likely to open up public space for God.

Chapter 4 argues that one of the most important trends in the modern West, the decoupling of wealth and life satisfaction, is orienting policy and public rhetoric towards a goal that has historically been firmly established in religious territory: the idea of well-being. Again, this fact alone, quite apart from the well-established links between religious belief and well-being, will extend the role of religious thinking into the public square.

Chapter 5 touches upon the variety of trends and ideas that have converged to bring the politics of identity centre stage today. It argues that well-formed and deeply-rooted religious identities will form an inescapable part of this identity politics, and that the best way of drawing the extremism that so often accompanies religious thinking is to include religious groups in public debate, forcing them to justify their convictions in publicly-accessible terms.

Chapter 6 concludes by touching on one other reason why religious involvement in public discourse is likely to increase in the future before exploring, albeit briefly, how we might "do God" in twenty-first century Britain.

The report is written from a Christian perspective and is, for the most part, about the role of Christianity in British public life. That said, it does at times address other religions and "religion" in general. It attempts to practise what it preaches by relying on public reason, using constructive rather than destructive arguments and adopting a tone of respect. Whether reasoning, arguments or tone succeed, the reader will judge.

introduction - references

1   The interview transcript can be found at http://news.bbc.co.uk/1/hi/uk_politics/4773874.stm

2   http://news.bbc.co.uk/1/hi/uk_politics/4773852.stm

3   http://news.bbc.co.uk/1/hi/uk_politics/4773124.stm

4   The full interview can be read at http://education.guardian.co.uk/schools/story/0,,1735857,00.html

5   See http://www.mirandagrell.com/?p=67

6   http://news.bbc.co.uk/1/hi/england/london/4398680.stm

7   http://www.telegraph.co.uk/news/main.jhtml?xml=/news/2005/06/09/ncrem09.xml

8   http://icwales.icnetwork.co.uk/0100news/0200wales/tm_objectid=14538849&method=
    full&siteid=50082&headline=charity-s-funds-cut-over-religious-links-name_page.html

9   http://www.publications.parliament.uk/pa/ld199697/ldhansrd/pdvn/lds05/text/50615-11.htm

10 http://www.worldnetdaily.com/news/article.asp?ARTICLE_ID=46970

11 http://news.bbc.co.uk/1/hi/education/4832072.stm

12 http://www.guardian.co.uk/Columnists/Column/0,,1657722,00.html

13 Julian Baggini, "The rise, fall and rise again of secularism" in *Public Policy Review* (PPR), Vol. 12,
    Issue 4, January - March 2006, p. 202

14 http://www.bbc.co.uk/radio3/speechanddrama/returnoffaith.shtml

15 Jonathan Fox, "World Separation of Religion and State Into the 21st Century"
    in *Comparative Political Studies*, Vol. 39 No. 5, June 2006, pp. 537-569

16 Quoted in John Coffey, "Secularisation: is it inevitable?" in Cambridge Papers Vol. 10, No. 1,
    March 2001

17 Sunder Katwala, "Faith in Democracy: The legitimate role of religion" in *PPR* 12.4, p. 245-250

why the reasons against "doing God" don't quite add up

For many years the British didn't need a reason for not "doing God".

British Prime Ministers of the twentieth century paid due lip service to their Anglican or occasionally nonconformist beliefs, but few openly admitted allowing their religious beliefs to fuel their politics, and certainly none to the extent of William Gladstone or Tony Blair. God, in Britain, was a frail, elderly relative, slightly embarrassing but a decent enough chap. He couldn't be taken seriously any more, but he still had a few uses. He could help maintain "family" unity at times of national ceremony or crisis, and perhaps even cajole the children into some kind of moral respectability. The rest of the time he could be "banished … upstairs to a religious House of Lords, and left … to mumble into his beard while we get on running the world by ourselves."[1]

If this was a slightly sad state of affairs, it was perfectly understandable. His frailty was down to a few nasty muggings in old age. Back in the early nineteenth century Ludwig Feuerbach had shown that he was a delusion. A little later Marx demonstrated that he was merely the result of mankind's economic and social alienation, and a few years after that Freud proved he was an infantile illusion resulting from our sense of helplessness.[2] If that wasn't enough, Charles Lyell, Charles Darwin and a host of German theologians showed that we should never have taken him at face value in the first place. No one could be expected to have survived such a series of brutal attacks unscathed. God might have somehow hung on, but he was a pale shadow of his former self, creeping around the public square and doing what he had always done, but without the self-confidence he had once possessed.

If the general public had more sympathy for this frail elderly relative than the intelligentsia, that was simply because they were ignorant. Education would disabuse them of their infantile notions. Secularisation was inevitable. Church attendance figures were, indeed, a little behind the intellectuals' trajectory, but the decline that began in the 1940s accelerated as the century continued and appeared inexorable as party-goers celebrated Jesus' 2,000th birthday.

It was because the British had got used to this state of affairs that they were so unprepared for the need to argue against "doing God". God's return was not quite "as shocking as hearing a knocking on a coffin lid at a funeral," as Julian Baggini has suggested, but it was still something of a surprise.[3] The feeble and slightly embarrassing old man who had been pacing about the house quietly mumbling to himself suddenly wanted to participate in family conversations and, what's more, to be taken seriously.

And it was perhaps because of this that arguments against "doing God" were so often so bad. Britain had no history of anti-clericalism on which sceptics might seize. Christianity had long been an obvious point of social cohesion, not to mention providing the vast bulk of welfare services before the state stepped in. Those who wished to eject God from the national conversation to which he had invited himself didn't have much to go on.

The result was that some highly intelligent and erudite individuals voiced arguments that they would have been the first to demolish had they fallen from opponents' lips. Thus, the philosopher, AC Grayling, wrote:

> All religions are such that if they are pushed to their logical conclusions … they will take the form of their respective fundamentalisms…[4]

And:

> We have the spectacle of the righteous writing letters of complaint about televised nudity, while from the factory next door tons of armaments are exported to regions of the world gripped by poverty and civil war.[5]

The need to resort to gross exaggerations, misrepresentations and caricatures of this kind does nothing so much as to betray the poverty of serious arguments. In the same article, Grayling argued:

> if anyone bothered to examine what a Christian … morality demanded, he would be amazed by its diametric opposition to what is regarded as normal and desirable now, and therefore by the degree of its irrelevance.[6]

Such reasoning – a moral code is irrelevant if it is radically different from whatever is currently regarded as normal – is so bad that it is astounding that anyone, let alone someone as clever as Grayling, could come up with it. This, as the equally atheistic Julian Baggini has remarked, was not so much secularism as theophobia.[7]

Grayling is certainly no worse than other intemperate secularists whose arguments against "doing God" often amount to little more than name-calling. Christianity is mere "superstition", faith a process of "non-thinking", God "a virus", religion the "root of all evil", religious people "cloth heads". In as far as religious arguments are ever actually examined, they are straw men, based either on single verses plucked from the Bible or Koran, shorn of their context, uncritically absorbed and then portrayed as the epitome of the religion in question, or, alternatively, on the grotesque, usually violent behaviour of individuals who are denounced by 99 per cent of the religions on whose behalf they purportedly act.

The tragedy in all this is that there are good arguments against religious involvement in the public square that religious advocates must address if they wish to "do God". They are simply lost when megaphoned into slogans and insults.

inflexible

Broadly speaking, such arguments fall into five categories, four of which will be examined here, with the fifth reserved for the next chapter. The first is that religiously-motivated engagement in the public square is inherently inflexible.

Politics is, at best, the art of the possible, or at worst, in JK Galbraith's words, the art of choosing between the disastrous and the unpalatable. Whatever else it might be, it is the arena for compromise, and religions don't like compromise. Indeed, the very word "compromise", which has positive connotations of cooperation and conciliation in the political arena, has negative ones of weakness and cowardice in the religious one.

This is a fair point, for which the behaviour of certain religious groups often provides supporting evidence. Yet, there is just as much counter-evidence, should we care to notice it. Ann Widdecombe, one of the most vociferously religious of all MPs, recounts how, when she first won her seat, she was faced with David Alton's private member's bill to reduce the upper time limit for abortion, from 28 to 18 weeks. This itself constituted a compromise of her (and others') beliefs, as did the prospect of exempting all unborn handicapped children in order for the bill to be passed at its second reading. This was anathema both to her and the bill's sponsors. Yet, as Widdecombe remarked in her 2006 Archbishop Worlock Memorial Lecture, it was a compromise worth making:

> An examination of the figures showed that of all abortions after the eighteenth week 8% were performed on grounds of handicap leaving 92 per cent performed for other reasons. I argued that if I were to be confronted with a shipwreck and a hundred drowning people, I would not refuse to save ninety-two for the sake of the eight I could not reach. We should, I believed, maximise the saving of unborn life rather than take an absolute position which would guarantee failure.[8]

In doing this, Widdecombe was doing no more than following core Catholic teaching. For example, John Paul II wrote in his encyclical *Evangelium Vitae*:

> when it is not possible to overturn or completely abrogate a pro-abortion law, an elected official, whose absolute personal opposition to procured abortion was well known, could licitly support proposals aimed at limiting the harm done by such a law and at lessening its negative consequences at the level of general opinion and public morality. This does not in fact represent an illicit cooperation with an unjust law, but rather a legitimate and proper attempt to limit its evil aspects.[9]

There are, of course, those, of religious and non-religious ideologies, for whom no compromise or even dialogue is tenable. However, by their own nature, they tend to exclude themselves from the debate. Those who are serious about their religious beliefs tend to be serious about the need to debate, negotiate and compromise.

inhuman

The second argument is closely related to the first: religiously-motivated engagement in the public square is inherently inhuman. This is not the random insult it might first appear. Instead, it is the well-justified observation that because religious beliefs are, by definition, oriented around transcendent principles, they can only result in relativising and thereby diminishing human concerns.

Christianity has its own particular response to this criticism – the incarnation validates human concerns in a way they might not otherwise be – but in truth, this it less a criticism of religion than of ideology in general. The millions sacrificed on Utopia's altar through the twentieth century remind us that literally god-less ideas are as dangerous as allegedly godly ones.

The fact remains, however, that even after a century of ideologically-motivated bloodshed, the alternative – of ideologically-free politics – is not obviously better. As we have begun to realise over recent years, public vision that shuns the glue of ideology is easily fragmented. Joined-up government is an impossibility if there is nothing with which to join it up. Similarly, politics that is determinedly anthropocentric, shunning causes for the sake of people, tends to devalue those things whose relevance to human flourishing is not immediate. Politics that sheds its ideological skin soon sheds any obligation to the common good and degenerates into a competition as to who can shout loudest in trying to optimise their personal interests.

Nowhere is this better seen than in the current debate over climate change. Politics that lacks the organising idea of the common good, not only devalues the invisible ecological sinks and services that make human flourishing possible, but also fragments any political response, so that government promotes public transport on the one hand and new airports on the other. In reality having an ideologically-motivated vision of the common good that transcends immediate human concerns is no bar to participation in public debate and may even be a qualification.

Martin Luther King's aphorism that "if a man hasn't discovered something he will die for, he isn't fit to live," has attained a dark shadow over recent years, but his point remains valid.[10] If there is nothing wider than me or my interests for which I will fight, we all end up inhabiting a smaller, more selfish world.

> *In reality having an ideologically-motivated vision of the common good that transcends immediate human concerns is no bar to participation in public debate and may even be a qualification.*

sectarian

The third serious argument against "doing God" is that religiously-motivated engagement in the public square is inherently sectarian. Religions are made up of people "bound together" by some idea of the divine and of human well-being. Such identities are highly motivated, non-negotiable and hard-edged. They alienate those beyond them, fracture public discourse and, most seriously, invest public debate with an ultimacy it can ill-afford.

This is bad for the public square and bad for religion. Thus, during the First World War, the German theologian, Alfred Uckley could say:

> God is the God of the Germans. Our battles are God's battles. Our cause is a sacred, a wholly sacred matter. We are God's chosen among the nations. That our prayers for victory will be heard is entirely to be expected, according to the religious and moral order of the world.[11]

Whilst Bishop Arthur Winnington-Ingram of London said:

> This is a Holy War. We are on the side of Christianity against anti-Christ … It is a Holy War, and to fight in a Holy War is an honour.[12]

Not only can bringing God into an already tense public square invest disagreements with ultimate significance, raising the stakes and turning a febrile situation into a bloody one, but it can make a mockery of religious belief.

This is an undeniably serious problem, to which advocates for "doing God" must pay equally serious attention. It is not, however, a *necessary* problem. At the same time as Alfred Uckley and Arthur Winnington-Ingram were preaching their bellicose sermons, the Archbishop of Canterbury, Randall Thomas Davidson, said:

> We believe, with an intensity beyond words, that there does exist what our opponents deny, a higher law than the law of any state, a deeper allegiance than can be claimed by any earthly Sovereign, and that in personal and national conduct alike we have to follow higher and more sacred principles of honour than any state law can enforce.[13]

Religiously-inspired public engagement need not be sectarian and can, in fact, be the opposite, not least if it takes seriously the belief articulated by the Catechism of the Catholic Church that:

> authority does not derive its moral legitimacy from itself … [but] is exercised legitimately only when it seeks the common good of the group concerned and if it employs morally licit means to attain it.[14]

That said, in much the same way as the previous criticism was more about a fear of ideology than a fear of religion, this one is more about a fear of difference than of religion *per se*. The motivating belief in universal human fraternity that has been central to the left for so many years is uncomfortable with anything, let alone anything as powerful as religion, that might act as a potential source of conflict. Difference divides and divisions kill.

Whilst this approach is admirable in theory, its logical extension in practice is that any who wish to participate in the public square must shed particular allegiances and any signs that hang there must be inclusive, in such a way as turns them into a rather insipid and uninspiring greywash.

This is what ultimately drives the annual round of "winterval" stories. Anything that hopes to inhabit the public square must not give offence to anyone who happens to be wandering around there. Hence the commendable desire to foster cohesion ends up in the rightly mocked absurdities of political correctness.

There is, however, another way, one that has become almost synonymous with the Chief Rabbi, Dr Jonathan Sacks' book, *The Dignity of Difference*. Sacks argues that, "there is no road to human solidarity that does not begin with moral particularity – by coming to know what it means to be a child, a parent, a neighbour, a friend. We learn to love humanity by loving specific human beings … The unity of God is to be found in the diversity of creation."[15] A diversity that makes life possible, interesting and dignified.

This is what the Catholic composer, James MacMillan, outlined in his speech, "Scotland's Shame", at the Edinburgh Festival in 1999, when he described how he dreamed of "a genuinely pluralistic democracy where differences are not just recognised and respected, but celebrated, nurtured and absorbed for the greater good."[16]

Fears that this can lead to sectarianism are undoubtedly justified, but need to be countered with evidence that this need not be the case. People of different creeds can and do mix. To take two recent examples:

Over half the election funding for the Christian People's Alliance, Britain's only explicitly religious political party of recent years, came from non-Christians: Hindus, Muslims, Sikhs, Jews and atheists, who appreciated the fact that the party was prepared to stand up for values that they shared.

In a debate in the House of Lords in 2006 on the role of the churches in the civic life of towns and cities, the Muslim peer, Lord Ahmed, spoke of his experience working with the church as a councillor in Rotherham.

> I worked with Father Matthew Joy when there were tensions between the communities in 1994-95. That was one of the most wonderful experiences, for a church leader, a local councillor and the local mayor all to be seen going together when there was tension to visit communities where we were able to give the impression that we can all work together to bring harmony and equality for our communities.
>
> We were able to get some funding from the Church Urban Fund to establish a centre there. With the local church leaders … we were able to establish an advice centre that was a partnership between local people - the Muslim community as well as the Christian community - and the local authority … It helped to empower the local community and to deal with deprivation.[17]

Such examples testify to the fact that a society can celebrate the dignity of religious difference without sacrificing social cohesion. But that such an endeavour is hard work and potentially dangerous, should be denied by nobody.

inaccessible

The fourth and most significant objection to religiously-motivated engagement in the public square is that it is inherently inaccessible. Ideas driven and justified by my religious belief system fragment public discourse and alienate those outside my tradition.

When Ann Widdecombe said in her Archbishop Derek Warlock Memorial Lecture, "the Catholic teaching on chastity before marriage is right despite a widespread view that it is impractical, old-fashioned and dispensable," one has every right to ask "Who says it is right?" or "How do you know?" If the answer is the "Holy Scriptures" or "the Pope says so", further public debate is stymied and the public square is divided. What about those who do not accept these as sources of authority?

All too often this point is raised for purely polemical purposes. As Jeremy Waldron has written:

> Secular theorists often assume that they know what a religious argument is like: they present it as a crude prescription from God, backed up with threat of hellfire, derived from general or particular revelation, and they contrast it with the elegant simplicity of a philosophical argument by Rawls (say) or Dworkin. With this image in mind, they think it obvious that religious argument should be excluded from public life.[18]

Thankfully this is not always the case, as Julian Baggini has shown:

> Take debates about abortion. A devout Catholic is obviously going to be strongly influenced by her religious beliefs on the subject, and when speaking in a civic forum, such as Parliament, these beliefs will come through. But, vitally, she must find some way of expressing them in terms that everyone can understand and appreciate. If she says, "we should not allow abortion because it is against the teachings of the Roman Catholic Church", she has failed to make an argument that has any purchase beyond her own faith. If she argues for the sanctity of human life in terms which are not specific to the tenets of Roman Catholicism, then she is making a contribution to the secular debate, even though at root her basic commitments are grounded in religion.[19]

The trick, he observes, is to "find a way of expressing [such beliefs] in universalist and not particularist terms." In this he follows (and quotes) John Rawls whose writings on public reason have been highly influential:

> Reasonable comprehensive doctrines, religious or non-religious, may be introduced in public political discussion at any time, provided that in due course proper political reasons – and not reasons given solely by comprehensive doctrines – are presented that are sufficient to support whatever the comprehensive doctrines are said to support.[20]

This is a sound argument with a good precedent in the Christian theological doctrine of accommodation. This argues that in order to make himself known to us, God speaks a language we can understand. It is surely not too much to ask Christians, or indeed those of any religion, to do the same?

Indeed, it is not, but there remains a wider question about who sets the terms of public discourse. Who defines what public reason is? We deceive ourselves if we say that public reason can be truly neutral and it is questionable, to put it mildly, that those principles that Rawls and others claim command universal assent actually do so. Nicholas Wolterstorff has observed that "it would take a good deal of exegetic industry to figure out what Rawls means by 'reasonable', and even more to figure our what he means by 'rational'."[21]

If we are to take seriously the arguments of Isaiah Berlin or Alister MacIntyre that core human values are genuinely plural or incommensurable – and not just because certain people deem certain texts to be revelatory and others don't – we are faced with a problem. Who decides what constitutes a proper political reason? Who says what goes?

After the example given above, Baggini goes on to argue that, "a secular discussion of human rights, for example, is couched in terms which both the religious and non-religious can accept." This might or might not be true, but it is, in either case, not without problems.

How do you respond to those who argue that unless the concept of human rights is opened up to anything that can suffer pain or distress, it is "speciesist" and thereby morally indefensible?[22] What about those who argue that the language of human rights predetermines the debate over issues in which one party, such as the unborn, is effectively voiceless?[23] What if, as Onora O'Neil argued in her 2002 Reith lectures, "too heavy an emphasis on human rights erodes precisely that civil society from which states (which are supposed to guarantee our human rights) draw their authority and power?"[24] What if the pragmatism that underpins the very concept of human rights becomes unable to deliver the goods in the long run and leaves the field open to those with less scrupulous, less admirable motives?[25]

None of these questions is intended to attack the concept "human rights" *per se* but merely to point out the problems that *any* form of public reason, however theoretically universal, will have if it attempts to provide the framework and vocabulary for public debate.

The purpose of all this is not to deter those who wish to foster truly inclusive public reason nor to allow those motivated by religious (and other) convictions to revert to self-referential validations and vocabulary. Indeed, it is to endorse John Rawls' idea that participation in the public square requires publicly accessible thinking.

However, this does not mean that what passes for public reason is either immutable or beyond challenge. In the same way as the Parekh report into *The Future of Multi-Ethnic Britain,* argued that "public life should recognise a wider range of cultural identities," and "mov[e] towards a much greater public recognition of difference – the rights of communities to live according to their own conception of the good life,"[26] so public reason should be open and even adaptable to reasoning that stands beyond its alleged boundaries. Put more simply, religious participation within the public square must accommodate itself to public reason, but public reason must be willing to accommodate itself to religious participation. As the theologian, Nigel Biggar, has argued:

> The engagement between theologians and non-theologians on matters of public concern need not be any less fruitful or any less capable of reaching a measure of agreement than engagements between different types of non-theologian whose views draw on conflicting anthropological or metaphysical convictions – say between communists and liberals, humanist globalisers and misanthropic ecologists, just war proponents and pacifists. The problem is not theology. The problem is not even metaphysics. The problem is that subscribers to world-views of all kinds – and no one is not a subscriber – sometimes prefer to bully rather than to reason together.[27]

It has been the contention of this chapter that, if one can get beyond the bullying to the reasoning, and listen to the voices behind the megaphones, one will hear good reasons against "doing God". Introducing religious groups, motivations, language and reasoning into the public square *is* dangerous, as all of the above can be inflexible, inhuman, sectarian and inaccessible.

None of these, however, is a sufficient or conclusive argument and, time and again, the reality of religiously-inspired public engagement betrays the nervous theory that argues against it. Nevertheless, each accusation is, in some way, valid, and those intent on "doing God" must be mindful of the words of warning that such arguments offer.

There is one final argument against "doing God". This comes from a whole different angle and deserves a chapter to itself, not so much because it is stronger than those discussed in this chapter – it is, in fact, rather weaker – but because it is the most widespread.

chapter 1 - references

1   NT Wright, "God and Caesar: Then and Now", Jubilee Reflections Lecture at Westminster Abbey

2   From the vast range of literature on this, see Alister McGrath, *The Twilight of Atheism: The Rise and Fall of Disbelief in the Modern World* (Rider & Co. 2004); AN Wilson, *God's funeral* (John Murray, 1999); Owen Chadwick, *The Secularisation of the European Mind in the Nineteenth Century* (CUP, 1978)

3   Julian Baggini, "The rise, fall and rise," *PPR* 12.4, p. 204

4   http://www.acgrayling.com/secular.html

5   http://www.acgrayling.com/Churches/church.html

6   http://www.acgrayling.com/Churches/church.html

7   Julian Baggini, "The rise, fall and rise," *PPR* 12.4, p. 207

8   Ann Widdecombe, Archbishop Worlock Memorial Lecture, 2006

9   John Paul II, *Evangelium Vitae*, sect. 73

10 Martin Luther King speaking in Detroit, 23 June 1963

11 Quoted in Michael Burleigh, *Earthly Powers* (Harper Collins, 2005), p. 445

12 Quoted in Burleigh, *Earthly Powers*, p. 450

13 Quoted in Burleigh, *Earthly Powers*, p. 442

14 *Catechism of the Catholic Church*, sects. 1902-1903

15 Jonathan Sacks, *The Dignity of Difference* (Continuum, 2002) p. 58

16 Quoted in The Parekh Report, *The Future of Multi-Ethnic Britain* (Profile Books, 2000), p. 242

17 Lord Ahmed, Hansard, 19 May 2006, Col. 534

18 Quoted in Nigel Biggar, "'God' in Public Reason" in *Studies in Christian Ethics* (SCE), Vol. 19 No. 1, p. 12

19 Julian Baggini, "The rise, fall and rise," *PPR* 12.4, p. 208

20 Quoted in Julian Baggini, "The rise, fall and rise," *PPR* 12:4, p. 208

21 Quoted in Biggar, "Public Reason," in *SCE* 19.1, p. 18

22 Richard Ryder, "All beings that feel pain deserve human rights," The *Guardian*, 6 August 2005: http://www.guardian.co.uk/animalrights/story/0,11917,1543799,00.html

23 See Meic Pearse, *Why the rest hates the West* (SPCK, 2003), pp. 72-74

24 Onora O'Neill, *A Question of Trust*, The 2002 Reith Lectures

25 Conor Gearty, *Can Human Rights Survive?: The Crisis of Authority*, Hamlyn Lectures 2005, Lecture 1

26 The Parekh Report, p. 242

27 Biggar, "Public Reason," in *SCE* 19.1, p. 17-18

God and Caesar

It is easy to get a sense of *déjà vu* when watching *Newsnight*.

That programme, and indeed all those that share a similar format, rehearse one particular scene with such peculiar regularity that it seems almost scripted.

The Church has published a report on inner city poverty or the treatment of asylum seekers or some such issue and the Bishop of Somewhere has been called up to explain and defend the conclusions. Questions are addressed and answers offered. Accusations are levelled and refuted. And then, about three-quarters of the way into the interview, the interviewer will almost invariably say something like, "There is a wider question here, isn't there? Should the Church really be getting involved in politics in this way? Aren't you in danger of mixing up the things of God with the things of Caesar?"

There it is. The Gospel according to St Matthew, chapter 22, verse 21, hacked out of context and dragged under the studio spotlight. The Temple is nowhere to be seen. The Pharisees and the Herodians have disappeared and Jesus himself is only lurking vaguely in the background. "Render unto Caesar the things which are Caesar's; and unto God the things which are God's."

> *Such ecclesiastical publications as might land a bishop in the Newsnight studio are seen as a bit "extra-curricular", brief diversions from the clergy's main roles of singing and wearing frocks in public.*

The idea that, according to true Christian theology, God and Caesar have nothing to do with one another has become strangely pervasive in the modern era. Such ecclesiastical publications as might land a bishop in the *Newsnight* studio are seen as a bit "extra-curricular", brief diversions from the clergy's main roles of singing and wearing frocks in public. Thus even the formidably erudite Diarmaid MacCulloch can write perplexingly in a review of Michael Burleigh's book, *Earthly Powers*:

Christianity's close association with power and politics is a curious lurch away from its founder Jesus, a poor man whose recorded pronouncements on the powerful are either jokes, parables or an emphatic statement, amid the fraught political situation of Palestine, that politics was nothing to do with him.[1]

That this represents a misunderstanding of Jesus, the Bible and the Christian Church is, to put it mildly, an understatement. As the political theologian, Oliver O'Donovan, has written:

> Rule out the political questions and you cut short the proclamation of God's saving power; you leave people enslaved where they ought to be set free from sin – their own and others.[2]

Christianity must be public in order to be itself. Although some maintain that religious people of all stripes should be allowed to practise their religion as long as it has no public presence, most recognise Christianity's essentially public nature.

There is often, however, a silent distinction between public and seriously public. It is the distinction between open-air carol services and prayers in Parliament, or between signs that hang outside churches and the "Faith in the City" report. This is not so much the distinction between the political and the public – public issues do not have to reach Westminster in order to be serious – as it is the distinction between what actually, meaningfully shapes our lives and what doesn't. And whereas the church can frolic around all it likes in its various fêtes and jamborees, its presence is not so welcome in the *Newsnight* studio.

"politics" and the Old Testament

Yet, as Rowan Williams argued in his 2004 Romanes Lecture:

> a religious life is a material life … it has to do with gesture, place, sound, habit … [and a] fundamental mistake is to consider belief itself, in its corporate religious context, as more or less exclusively a mental event.

The Israel of the Bible was a public body. Its laws had much to say about personal piety and just as much about economic, social and political justice. Its Hymns Ancient and Modern, the *Psalms*, sang a great deal about personal despair and joy, and just as much about YHWH being king, a "political" statement, if ever there was one. The Prophets, or those whose words made it into the canon, warned the people about the consequences of personal sinfulness, *and* of their handling of asylum seekers, the poor, the law courts, income distribution and welfare provision. They were also not afraid to adopt nakedly "political" roles, whether resisting royal acquisitiveness, forming a national resistance movement, or publicly enacting the fate of the capital city. In all this they were intended to be "a light to the nations"

(Isaiah 51.4), a nation of whom others would say, "surely this is a wise and understanding people". (Deuteronomy 4.6)

None of this means that the Hebrew Bible was a political book as we might understand the term. Indeed, it is notable not so much for the political template it offers to achieve those ends, as the absence of one. Throughout, there is a reluctance to make direct connections with any concrete form of political order.

The need for some form of human mediation of God's rule was recognised, but how that should be organised and, in particular, whether it should be through an individual, was a matter for debate. In O'Donovan's words:

> The debate was comparable to that which emerged in modern political thought in the terms of "separation of powers". Can sovereignty that belongs to a spiritual body (whether God or the people) be exercised whole and entire by one representative person, or must it be diffused among different offices?[3]

Not surprisingly, that representative, the king, was a controversial figure, and the office of kingship painfully ambiguous. On the one hand, many psalms celebrated the rule of the king as God's anointed. On the other, there was little doubt about the dangers of concentrating power in this way. The law placed severe restrictions on the king's power (Deuteronomy 17.14-20) but to little avail. As the prophet, Samuel, warned:

> This is what the king who will reign over you will do: He will take your sons and make them serve with his chariots and horses … He will take your daughters to be perfumers and cooks and bakers. He will take the best of your fields and vineyards and olive groves and give them to his attendants. He will take a tenth of your grain and of your vintage and give it to his officials and attendants … He will take a tenth of your flocks, and you yourselves will become his slaves. (1 Samuel 8.11-18)

The generally lamentable history of the kings proved the prophet right. Six hundred or so years before Jesus' birth, the nation was conquered and sent into exile.

the coming of the Kingdom

By the time Jesus was born, the people were back in the land but still, essentially, in exile. A succession of empires – the Babylonian, Persian, Greek and then Roman – had ruled over them with more or less crassness. Even when Judea was made a province in its own right, following a rebellion in Jesus' youth, its government by a series of procurators did not improve the matter. The kingship of God of which the Psalmists had sung remained something of a dream.

The response of Jesus' contemporaries to this was diverse. Some were willing to cooperate with their Roman overlords while others advocated wholesale and, if necessary, violent confrontation. The situation was tense, oscillating between open revolt and brutal reprisal.

Into this tinderbox walked a young, lower-class, Jewish unknown claiming that the time had come. "The kingdom of God is near. Repent and believe the good news." (Mark 1.15) Whatever else this meant, it was not simply a promise of inner peace. In the words of NT Wright, Bishop of Durham:

> "Kingdom of God" was not a vague phrase, or a cipher with a general religious aura. It had nothing much, at least in the first instance, to do with what happened to human beings after they died. The reverent periphrasis "kingdom of heaven", so long misunderstood by some Christians to mean "a place, namely heaven, where saved souls go to live after death", meant nothing of the sort in Jesus' world: it was simply a Jewish way of talking about Israel's god becoming king. [4]

In much the same way, "repentance" was not primarily about saying sorry for one's personal peccadilloes and "belief" was not a call to deploy philosophical arguments for the existence of God. The forgiveness of sins that Jesus offered was not only the absolution of individual misdemeanour, but also a way of indicating that Israel's exile was over. Jesus' appropriation of the phrase, the Son of Man, so commonly thought to have something to do with Jesus' common humanity, meant something rather different. "No [contemporary] could hear this without understanding that imperial oppression was to be replaced by the rule of the saints, the restored Israel which would exercise a humane authority granted it by God."[5] As far as Jesus and his first followers were concerned, the Kingdom had arrived in and through Jesus himself. If this was not a public message, nothing was.

Precisely what this entailed is beyond the scope of this report, but two observations are worth making. Firstly, the Kingdom was a public affair just as much, if not more than a private one. It offered rest for the weary and comfort for the mourners but much more. It promised a life in which weakness rather than strength commanded respect; personal generosity exceeded public expectation; forgiveness starved vengeance of oxygen; strangers were welcomed rather than tolerated; peacemakers celebrated over warriors; and the poor freed from the system that enslaved them. It was, in short, a kingdom of love, in which everything was shaped around the desire to seek the fullness and flourishing of the other.

Secondly, it was a risky business. As NT Wright has written:

> Anyone announcing the kingdom of YHWH was engaging in serious political action. Anyone announcing the kingdom but explicitly opposing armed

resistance was engaging in doubly serious political action: not only the occupying forces, but all those who gave allegiance to the resistance movement, would be enraged.[6]

Just how risky this was can be seen in the language that St Paul chose to write to the first Christian communities. In the same way as Jesus' words have often been spiritualised into a message of personal piety, Paul's talk of righteousness and justification have been understood, if at all, as referring solely to the arcane and convoluted process whereby individual believers achieve this state of personal holiness. Once again, this is, at best, a partial truth. In reality, "almost the whole vocabulary of salvation in the New Testament has a political pre-history of some kind: 'salvation' … 'justification', 'peace', 'faithfulness', 'faith', and above all the 'Kingdom of God'."[7]

As far as Paul's world was concerned the emperor was saviour. It was he who was "son of god", claiming the title on his predecessor's death. It was the Republic that had underwritten justice (elevating Iustitia to an official goddess) and the *Pax Romana* that was the guarantor of peace. The "gospel" or "good news" was the annunciation of precisely these themes.

Thus, pretty much everything Paul wrote was public and risky. If Jesus was the world's Lord, Caesar was not. If Jesus' story was the good news, Caesar's was not. If Christians' citizenship was in heaven, it was not here. If their loyalty lay to Christ, it did not lie, at least in the first instance, with Caesar. It was now Jesus who offered peace and security, an imperial idiom, not Caesar. It was now Jesus' *parousia* (literally "appearance" but often translated "Second Coming") that mattered, not Caesar's. And it was Jesus who now ruled by means of the cross and not Caesar.

Given these incendiary implications, it is hardly surprising that Paul and his fellow travellers aroused some hostility. When an angry mob in Thessalonica, unable to find Paul and Silas, dragged one of their friends, Jason, into the street and accused him of "defying Caesar's decrees, [by] saying that there is another king, one called Jesus," they had, at least, grasped the content of Paul's preaching. (Acts 17.7)

Nor is it surprising that many early Christian writers were concerned with showing that Christians were not quite so much a threat to social order as their critics accused them of being. "When you hear that we look for a kingdom," Justin Martyr wrote in the early second century, "you uncritically suppose that we speak of a human one; whereas we speak of that with God."[8] Christians might have been a sect, but they were not, according to the slightly later writer, Tertullian, sectarian:

> The reason for prohibiting [our] associations clearly lay in forethought for public order – to save the state from being torn into parties… [but] we… have no need

to combine; nothing is more foreign to us than the state. One state we know, of which all are citizens – the universe.[9]

Such apologies were more than just rhetoric. The early Christians were not anarchists. They did not simply wish to overthrow the authorities, still less to live with no earthly authority in place. "Earthly rule … has been appointed by God for the benefit of the nations … so that under the fear of it men may not eat each other up," wrote Irenaeus of Lyons in the second century.[10] "I will pay honour to the emperor not by worshipping him but by praying for him," wrote Theophilus of Antioch a few years later.[11]

In this they were conscious inheritors of the first Christians, who were careful to emphasise their respect for "the powers that be". "Everyone must submit himself to the governing authorities, for there is no authority except that which God has established," Paul wrote to the Christians in Rome. (Romans 13.1) "I urge … that requests, prayers, intercession and thanksgiving be made for everyone," he wrote to his younger companion, Timothy, especially "for kings and all those in authority, that we may live peaceful and quiet lives in all godliness and holiness." (1 Timothy 2.1)

If this seems confusing – Christianity was an open challenge to the existing public system, but advocated political obedience – it goes some way to explaining the confused perceptions with which this chapter started. Moreover, because both strands in Christian thinking can be traced back to the question Jesus was asked on the Temple mount, it is hardly surprising that this encounter above any other is used to argue for privatised Christianity.

The question was, of course, a trick one. NT Wright explains:

> The great revolution of Jesus' boyhood days had been a tax revolt against Rome, and Rome had put it down brutally, with thousands of young Jews being crucified. Refusal of Rome's taxes was from then on a standard feature of any would-be Kingdom-of-God movement. For Jesus to say "Yes, pay the tax," would have been interpreted as saying "I'm not serious about God's Kingdom". But for him to incite people not to pay was just the sort of charge that would get him killed by the Romans.[12]

Jesus' response was masterly. His phrase, "Give back to Caesar what is Caesar's", echoes the words of Mattathias in 1 Maccabees (a book that charts the last great successful Jewish rebellion) as he is telling his sons to get ready for revolution. Jesus' audience is certain to have heard the anti-imperial sentiments beneath the phrase.

Yet, anti-imperial sentiments are not the same as a revolutionary rallying cry. As every God-fearing first-century Jew would have known, "The earth is the Lord's, and everything in it." (Psalms 24.1) Caesar is entitled to collect the taxes owed him, but they, he and everything else were owed to God. If this makes Jesus appear indifferent to the plight of his people, it is not because he didn't care about Roman rule. It was because he believed that in him and with the coming of the Kingdom, everything changed. He refused to advocate open rebellion because that was not the way of the Kingdom.

Oliver O'Donovan uses a telling example to explain this:

> Imagine an official of the Russian Government in October 1991, confronted with some demand from the foundering Soviet authorities. "This is ridiculous!" he thinks to himself. "We will be running that ourselves by next week!" Yet to display open contempt would give the impression that the new authorities did not believe in constitutional government at all. So confident is he of the shape of the coming order, that he has no need of an insolent posture to assert it against the order that is vanishing. Jesus, similarly, believed that a shift in the locus of power was taking place, which made social institutions that had prevailed to that point anachronistic. His attitude to them was neither secularist nor zealot: since he did not concede that they had any future, he gave them neither dutiful obedience within their supposed sphere of competence nor the inverted respect of angry defiance. [13]

Christian secularism

It is by means of this thinking – and not without irony – that we arrive at secularism and the concept of the secular public square. The word "secular", originally from a Latin word meaning "generation" or "age" was adopted in early Christian writings to mean "this age" or, more precisely, "confined to this present age that is passing away". The secular was Christianity's gift to the world, denoting a public space in which authorities should be respected but could legitimately be challenged and could never accord to themselves absolute or ultimate significance.

This was something the early Church understood well. In Peter's letter to Christians scattered around the eastern Mediterranean, he told them they were "a people belonging to God", but that didn't mean they owed nothing to the earthly rulers under whom they lived. On the contrary, they were to "submit … to every authority instituted among men: whether … king … or … governors, who … punish those who do wrong and to commend those who do right." (1 Peter 2.13-14) But this, in turn, does not mean that such kings and governors are, by definition, right, and Peter proceeds to advise his readers what they should do when injustice is done. Similarly, the anonymous second-century writer of the Letter to Diognetus, explains to his reader:

> Though [Christians] are residents at home in their own countries, their behaviour

there is more like that of transients; they take their full part as citizens, but they also submit to anything and everything as if they were aliens … their days are passed on earth, but their citizenship is above in the heavens. They obey the prescribed laws, but in their own private lives they transcend the laws.[14]

The Old Testament's nervousness about a single individual mediating God's rule for the people crystalises into the Christian denial that any particular political order is sacred, and, in doing so, produces the concept of a secular public square of which we are inheritors.

But we are only inheritors of it, as Rowan Williams has argued, because we are inheritors of the Judaeo-Christian intellectual foundations on which it is built. A belief in the provisionality and impermanence of political power, which forms the basis of political liberalism, is Christendom's legacy to the modern world. Accordingly:

Western modernity and liberalism are at risk when they refuse to recognise that they are the way they are because of the presence in their midst of that partner and critic which speaks of "alternative citizenship" – the Christian community … the distinctively European style of political argument and debate is made possible by the Church's persistent witness to the fact that states do not have ultimate religious claims on their citizens.[15]

Societies that forget this seminal Christian vision of "dual citizenship" stumble towards absolutism, either in the form of religious theocracy or state totalitarianism, in such a way as dehumanises its own people. This is an error into which theophobic secularism can fall.

When the Church is regarded as an enemy to be overcome or a private body that must be resolutely excluded from public debate, liberal modernity turns itself into a fixed and absolute thing, another pseudo-religion, in fact … Unless the liberal state is engaged in a continuing dialogue with the religious community, it loses its essential liberalism. It becomes simply dogmatically secular…[16]

By concluding in this way we have consciously moved from a negative argument – defending Christianity against the largely baseless accusation that it is an inherently private phenomenon – towards a positive one – that the secular public square, properly understood, is a Christian legacy and one that requires an ongoing Christian presence to remain true to itself.

As positive arguments for "doing God" go this is important, but it is far from conclusive. The following chapters will explore three more substantial reasons, which, in combination, suggest that allowing God to participate in Caesar's public square is not just advisable but, in fact, inevitable.

chapter 2 - references

1   Diarmaid MacCullogh, "Holy and Profane" in the *Guardian*, 22 October 2005
    http://books.guardian.co.uk/reviews/history/0,,1597839,00.html

2   Oliver O'Donovan, *The Desire of the Nations* (CUP, 1996), p. 3

3   Oliver O'Donovan, *Nations*, p. 52

4   NT Wright, *Jesus and the Victory of God* (SPCK, 1996), p. 202

5   Oliver O'Donovan, *Nations*, p. 90

6   NT Wright, *Victory*, p. 296

7   Oliver O'Donovan, *Nations*, p. 22

8   Justin's *First Apology* in O'Donovan and O'Donovan, *From Irenaeus to Grotius: A Sourcebook in Christian Political Thought* (Cambridge: Eerdmans, 1999), p. 12

9   Tertullian's *Apology* in O'Donovan and O'Donovan, *From Irenaeus* p. 26

10 Irenaeus of Lyon's *Against Heresies* in O'Donovan and O'Donovan, *From Irenaeus* p. 17

11 Theophilus of Antioch's *To Autolycus* in O'Donovan and O'Donovan, *From Irenaeus* p. 14

12 NT Wright, "God and Caesar"

13 Oliver O'Donovan, *Nations*, p. 92

14 "Letter to Diognetus" in A Louth (ed.) *Early Christian Writings: The Apostolic Fathers* (Penguin Books, 1968; rev. 1987), p. 144-145

15 Rowan Williams, "Religion, culture, diversity and tolerance – shaping the new Europe," address at the European Policy Centre, Brussels, 7 November 2005

16 Rowan Williams, European Policy Centre address

the return of civil society

Once upon a time there was only civil society and most of it was Christian.

Most Victorians looked upon the state as an "artificial contrivance, useful in punishing sinners, but incapable of redemptive action."[1] Social problems were the result of individual, moral failings; their remedies lay in personal reformation. Government action stifled and obstructed domestic, community and religious life whence social salvation came. "The individual, not as ratepayer but as fellow-sufferer, was responsible for the cares of the world."[2] The result was a civil society, the space between rulers and ruled populated by independent, voluntary and charitable organisations, which was unlike anything Britain had previously seen.

Victorian civil society was extraordinarily dense, with the different Christian denominations dominating "welfare provision". Each had its own special interests and between them they ran literally thousands of charity schools, ragged schools, Sunday schools, mothers' meetings, soup kitchens, maternity charities, crèches, blanket clubs, coal clubs, clothing clubs, boot clubs, provident clubs, slate clubs, medical clubs, lending libraries, holiday funds, penny banks, saving banks, visiting societies, temperance societies and pension societies.

Between two-thirds and three-quarters of British working class had achieved a basic level of literacy by 1840, primarily due to the efforts of the Sunday schools.[3] By 1865, various denominations had set up over 600 ragged schools for destitute children, contributing as much to social welfare as to education.[4] By 1889, the Church of England alone counted over 47,000 district visitors in England and Wales, a number that rose to 74,000 by 1910.[5] By one estimate, evangelicals ran about three in four voluntary societies in the latter half of the nineteenth century.[6] According to the 42nd report of the Charity Commission published in 1895:

> The latter half of the 19th century will stand second in respect of the greatness and variety of Charities created within its duration, to no other half-century since the Reformation.[7]

As has sometimes been observed, the sheer number of such voluntary and charitable associations thwarted revolutionary theorists who predicted the collapse of the social order and saved the nation from a social revolution like those enjoyed on the continent.[8]

As the nineteenth century progressed, and in spite of many eminent Victorian opinions, the state gained a greater role in social service provision. Initially, this was limited to financial assistance and legislation for basic welfare issues, such as sanitation and factory life, but eventually state welfare provision became the norm.

Public opinions were changing. Assumptions about poverty were shifting with growing awareness of its systemic and economic causes. Technological advances began to demand large-scale medical responses and an increasingly professionalised workforce. Ever more parents were in favour of comprehensive education, discontinuing their subscriptions to the voluntary schools as they rallied to the board schools. The rapidly growing and urbanising population revealed a woeful lack of co-ordination between charities. Books like Charles Booth's *The Life and Labour of the People of London* and experiences such as the Boer and First World Wars revealed to the nation that the current system of voluntary provision simply wasn't delivering the goods, and that charities would never deliver on their promise of social regeneration.

All this, combined with the work of the *Luftwaffe,* which, in AJP Taylor's memorable phrase, acted as "a powerful missionary for the welfare state", won the debate.[9] A people's war demanded a people's peace, as William Beveridge remarked. The welfare state, a term originally popularised by William Temple, then Archbishop of York, was born.[10]

the state and civil society

It was born into, and to some extent created, a period of great optimism. The warfare state of history had finally given way to the welfare state of the future.[11] Whereas the Victorians had thought that poverty could only be ameliorated, the New Elizabethans knew that it would be abolished. An opinion poll in 1948 reported that over 90 per cent thought there was no longer any role for charity in Britain.[12] As Douglas Jay, financial secretary to the Treasury in Clement Attlee's post-war government, famously said, "In the case of nutrition and health, just as in the case of education, the gentlemen in Whitehall really do know better what is good for the people than the people know themselves."

There were words of palliation. Herbert Morrison said he did not wish to destroy voluntary effort that was "fundamental to the health of a democratic society".[13] Clement Attlee claimed that, "we shall always have alongside the great range of public services, the voluntary services which humanise our national life and bring it down from the general to the particular."[14]

And Beveridge himself wrote in his book, *Voluntary Action*:

> The making of a good society depends not on the State but on citizens, acting individually or in free association with one another, acting on motives of various kinds – some selfish, others unselfish, some narrow and material, others inspired by love of man and love of God. The happiness or unhappiness of the society in which we live depends upon ourselves as citizens, not only the instruments of political power which we call the State.[15]

But the spirit of the age was better captured by Richard Crossman, Secretary of State for Health and Social Security in the late 1960s, who observed that to radical socialists philanthropy was "an odious expression of social oligarchy and churchy bourgeois attitudes" and "do-gooding a word as dirty as philanthropy".[16]

The optimism did not survive the oil crisis. A cash-strapped government placed spending limits on state welfare provision, and helped revive an interest in the voluntary sector. At the same time, the welfare state faced mounting criticism for its bureaucratic inefficiency and, ironically, for patronising and infantilising welfare recipients – the same criticism that had been levelled so powerfully at the charitable sector.[17] The emerging New Right reverted to the language of freedom, choice, independence, voluntary endeavour and personal virtues, often wrapping them up in colourful Victoriana.

Yet Margaret Thatcher's Victorianism was highly selective. It offered few incentives to giving and passed (or tried to pass) legislation, such as the liberalisation of credit laws or Sunday trading, which would have scandalised her Victorian predecessors. More pointedly, much had changed. "[Thatcher's] sentiments were being voiced in a world that had lost its Christian underpinning. [Her] millionaires, unlike the Colmans, Rathbones, or Cadburys of the past, had other things to spend their money on than their fellow citizens."[18] A once rich civil society was a shadow of itself. Critics cited William Gladstone who had said in 1856, "the day you sanction compulsory rating for the purpose of education you sign the death warrant of voluntary exertions."[19]

Following the collapse of communism and the re-invention of the British Labour party five years later, however, it was clear in which direction the nation was headed. Civil society emerged as central to the business of government and, perhaps not surprisingly given its history, it dragged God back into the public square beside it.

the state of civil society

When Robert Putnam published his book, *Bowling Alone: The Collapse and Revival of American Community* in 2001, he alerted many to the dangerously low levels of social capital in America.[20] Subtle differences between US and UK culture – not least in the existence of a substantial welfare state – begged the question as to whether the British community life was on the same path towards disintegration. Numerous studies later, the consensus of opinion tends to be "No, but…".

Charles Pattie, Patrick Seyd and Paul Whiteley conclude their substantial study, *Citizenship in Britain: Values, Participation and Democracy*, by saying:

> the British public are … still active members of their communities, engaged in a wide range of both formal and informal activities … Britain at the start of the 21st century still enjoys a civic culture.[21]

There is, however, a "but…" in their conclusions. Britons remain "atomised citizens", those institutions that support collective action, such as political parties, are much weakened, and much participation is now either individualistic or of the "cheque book" variety, which essentially "involves … sub-contracting out one's participation to someone else".[22]

Britain, they conclude, is "divided between a well-connected group of citizens with prosperous lives and high levels of civic engagement and other groups whose networks, associational life and involvement is very limited." The consequence of this is that "non-participants are likely to be marginalised or ignored, since the electoral incentives are for parties to focus on participants".[23]

A similar study for the London School of Economics found that "formal participation in voluntary organisations and political engagement are [sic] increasingly concentrated in the middle and upper middle classes," that "levels of generalised social trust have levelled out and remain low," and "membership [of voluntary organisations] is increasingly being considered to be a product, for which certain benefits are received, rather than a commitment of support or involvement." "Britain," the authors concluded "may have experienced a decline in 'social capital' strikingly similar to that of the United States."[24]

One of the findings of the *Citizenship in Britain* study was that those individuals who regarded themselves as belonging to a particular religion (a notoriously "weak" grouping, as the 2001 National Census reminded us) often exhibited atypical characteristics. Such people recorded comparatively high levels of interpersonal trust, of trust in the police, of respect for the law and of a citizen's duty to vote. They also recorded higher than average levels of group membership, of engagement in informal activities, of political participation and of time "donation".[25]

This general outline of the particular contribution made by religious groups to civil society is being filled out by a growing number of studies. The 2003 report, *Faith in England's Northwest*, produced by the Northwest Development Agency examined "the contribution made by faith communities to civil society in the region". It surveyed more than 2,300 faith communities, encompassing 9 religions, and identified more than 5,000 significant "non-worship" projects involving over 45,000 volunteers.[26] The 2005 companion report, *Faith in England's Northwest: Economic Impact Assessment,* estimated that those volunteers contributed around 8.1 million volunteer hours per annum (the equivalent of 4,815 full-time jobs), with the financial value of this contribution being between £61 and £65 million each year.[27]

Another study, *Faith in the East of England,* recorded a similarly "enormous range of activities supported by worshipping communities … from the 'traditional' such as visiting the sick (80 per cent of faith groups do this) and running lunch clubs (36 per cent) to the more innovative such as IT training (7 per cent) and environmental groups (11 per cent)." The report estimated that the value of faith community volunteer work to the region was around £30 million per annum. The report also remarked that "most secular organisations interviewed had positive experiences of working with faith communities," and that "the concern that public resources granted may be used for proselytising purposes will usually be unfounded."[28]

Other reports point in the same direction.[29] According to the Church Life Profile 2001, members of the Church of England contribute 23.2 million hours' voluntary service each month in their local communities.[30] According to the Charity Commission, there are more than 22,000 religious charities working in England and Wales today, and the number is growing. In 2005, some 16.5 per cent of the 5,000 charities that registered were religious. Overall, the 2003 Home Office Citizenship Survey, *People, Families and Communities* calculated that a quarter of regular churchgoers, or around a million people, are involved in voluntary community service outside the church, concluding that "people who follow a religion were significantly more likely to be trustful or to formally volunteer."[31]

It should not (but regrettably will) need saying at this point that none of this is to suggest that those who do not belong to a religious group do not contribute to social capital. Although these surveys point to the disproportionate contribution to civil society made by faith groups, neither the surveys themselves nor the religious groups they study claim that non-religious groups fail to make a crucial contribution to civil society. This point was made explicitly in the Commission on Urban Life and Faith's report, *Faithful Cities:*

> We are not saying that only people or communities of faith have anything to offer in the making of good cities. We pay tribute to the thousands of people who would not claim – and in some cases would shun – association with religion or faith, yet who selflessly work for the common good. We also want to recognise that there are many people of faith who choose to put their talents and energy at the disposal of secular organisations and institutions, rather than through specifically religious initiatives. It is all to the good.[32]

faith in civil society

The sheer extent of the religious contribution to civil society – from large organisations, like the Children's Society or Barnado's to rather smaller ones like the Eden project in Manchester to the Eastside project in Newham – means that "faith" cannot help but be a significant factor in the public square. There are, however, four particular reasons over and above the simple volume of "faith-based" voluntary activity that makes God's presence in the public square particularly important.

Firstly, religious involvement in civil society is almost always group-based. There are some examples of individuals starting and running projects, such as the three Roman Catholic nuns who moved into a notoriously deprived area of Wolverhampton to serve the community, or the two Christian women from Hull who set up a drop-in centre for sex workers, but for the most part, religious participation is group participation. This is important in so far as it counters the increasingly atomised and consumerist approach to civil participation, an approach that, according to the *Citizenship in Britain* study, is fraught with danger:

> The importance of parties and encompassing representative interest groups is that they help to aggregate interests in society. In a world of special interest groups or narrow advocacy groups, actors seek benefits for the particular constituencies they represent while at the same time trying to avoid paying costs … In a fragmented, individualistic political system no one has an incentive to accept costs whereas everyone has an incentive to seek benefits. The risk is that policy-making will become gridlocked by ever-increasing demands for particularistic benefits alongside a growing reluctance of society to pay for those benefits … society needs encompassing groups like the mainstream political parties, or large trade unions in which demands for benefits have to be matched with a willingness to share the costs of collective action … The growth of atomised citizenship runs the risk of a growth of policy fragmentation and policy failure.[33]

Whatever else their motivations might be, such religiously - inspired civic engagement is not about *me*. As Rowan Williams said in a House of Lords' debate on the role of the churches in the civic life of towns and cities:

> Intentional communities which appeal to motivations beyond individual profit or short-term popularity have a unique role in galvanising urban, and of course not only urban, populations towards taking the kind of corporate responsibility for their future that they will need if change is to last.[34]

In this alone, faith-based civic activity provides a crucial counterbalance to "cheque book citizenship".

Secondly, and closely linked to this reason, such voluntary activity not only extends beyond the boundaries of the participating community, but it is commonly focused on those in greatest need. "Faith communities are extensively involved in providing services for older people, children and more deprived neighbourhoods in the [Nothwest] region ... [and] can help those working for regeneration, social inclusion or sustainable development to reach out to many of those who could be defined as 'hard to reach'."[35]

> *Whatever else their motivations might be, such religiously - inspired civic engagement is not about **me**.*

In a similar vein, the *Faith in the East of England* report recoded how a fifth of the faith-group respondents they interviewed worked with homeless people, a third with food distribution, 16 per cent provided assistance to those abusing alcohol, and 11 per cent to those abusing drugs. Nearly a third ran projects designed for unemployed adults, and nearly a quarter for people seeking to improve their skills. The report added that:

> Major beneficiary groups are children (86% of respondents had child-focused services) and the elderly (82%). Families under stress, one-parent families, single people and others who may be disadvantaged or vulnerable (disabled people: 45%; those with mental health difficulties: 37%; or learning difficulties: 36%) are well represented. This targeting also reflects an anti-discrimination agenda amongst many faith groups, which is emphasised by the fact that other key beneficiaries of projects are people from black and minority ethnic groups (36% of projects work with these) and to a lesser extent from gay and lesbian groups (15%).[36]

Not only do religious groups contribute significantly to social capital through their voluntary activities, but they do so where it is most needed.

Thirdly, such groups are very often in it for the long haul. This point applies to various denominations' existing church networks in general and to the Church of England's parish structure in particular. Not only is the volunteering that springs from these sources there, on the ground, locally owned, locally managed, and available to all, but it is there "regardless of the volatile chemistry of demography and property values".[37] In Rowan Williams' words:

> they speak of a commitment and an availability of social capital that is not likely to be withdrawn when things get difficult. In a world of time-limited grants and often desperate scrambling to create leadership and management structures that will survive the somewhat breathless rhythms of funding regimes, they allow a longer view. They are likely to be there still when particular schemes end in wreckage.[38]

Fourthly, religious groups are very often involved not simply as another special interest group but as potential brokers between interest groups. Nowhere is this more evident than in the presence and use of church buildings. The way in which such facilities are used by local communities is not only financially significant. The *Faith in England's Northwest: Economic Impact Assessment* estimated that "premises made available by faith communities in the Northwest generate between £574,755 and £811,472 per annum".[39] They are also socially important.

Survey after survey shows that the vast majority of people, irrespective of religious persuasion, appreciate the presence of such buildings in their neighbourhood.[40] Moreover, a surprising number of them use these facilities, sometimes through personal attendance at occasional services and sometimes through other community activities that use church halls and rooms.

This use by all sectors of the community points beyond the buildings themselves to how religious groups, in particular the established church, can act as a body that provides "a necessary space in the social map beyond the stand-offs of rival bids and concerns".[41] Rowan Williams recounts how when, sharing a platform in Merthyr Tydfil with the then secretary of the Welsh TUC, he was introduced as a speaker from a church which was there "to speak for all those who did not have certain kinds of protection – the protection of trade unions, the protection of regular incomes, the protection of party interests of one sort or another." The Church was the group" that had the freedom to hold other groups together because it was not simply fighting its own corner." It was, he remarks, one of the defining insights of his time as Bishop of Monmouth.[42]

One doesn't need to be a member of the National Secular Society to recognise that this isn't always the case. Nevertheless, the use of church buildings and the warm affection that the Church of England retains in the mind of a largely non-church-attending public testifies to the fact that it is truer than we might otherwise think.

outstanding questions

Overall, the extensive and particular contributions that religious groups in general, and the churches, in particular, make to civil society not only bring religion back into the public square but place it somewhere near the middle.

This has been recognised by government in a number of ways, many of which lurk unnoticed in the shadows of the larger question of the role of faith groups in education. Starting with the Inner Cities Religious Council (ICRC) in 1992, successive governments have sought to put the faith groups' role in building civil society onto an official footing, most recently through the Cohesion and Faiths Unit, in the Home Office's the Race, Cohesion and Faith Directorate.[43]

None of this is to suggest that there remain no problems. Oddly, however, the most obvious one, discussed in chapter 1, that such faith-driven activity can be sectarian, does not appear to have been much of an issue to date (a further example of reality betraying theory). The very fact that these religiously-motivated activities tend to focus on shared ethical objectives – educating children, treating addictions, uniting families, protecting the elderly, building community life – means that, if anything, such religiously-inspired work unites rather than divides religious groups. Many voluntary bodies are started, managed and owned by single groups, for all the obvious reasons of vision and administration, but it is not uncommon to see faith groups working together towards shared objectives.

More serious is the question mark that government funding and regulation raises for religious organisations. Government's contribution to philanthropic work has risen from about 10 per cent in the mid-1980s to around 35 per cent today, and, in doing so, has raised doubts about the independent, voluntary and motivational ethos of religious charitable groups.[44] Put simply, the more strings that tie them to the state's purse, the less independent, voluntary and overtly religious they have the freedom to be.

But this is also a problem for government. The 2003 Joseph Rowntree Foundation report, *"Faith" in Urban Regeneration?*, highlighted the particular difficulties that many faith groups faced in dealing with local authorities that, they felt, were either ignorant, suspicious or overtly antagonistic in their dealings with them.[45] The later JRF report, *Faith as Social Capital*, concluded that:

> local authorities, primary care trusts, police authorities and other such agencies have to develop a much more sophisticated understanding of faith communities with much closer relationships if latent social capital is to be used effectively.[46]

On occasion this unwillingness to engage with the reality of religiously-inspired charitable work can reach comic levels. One Christian minister recounts how he and other faith group leaders were asked to go away and come back with a "faith-sector" position on a particular issue. He replied that they would do that as soon as the officials with whom they were talking gave them the official "political sector" position on the same issue.[47]

Just as religious charities face questions about whether they can remain true to their vision whilst tied to official purse strings, government needs to think about whether it can "partner" with such groups in the way it is keen to, without permitting them a greater level of independence and recognising their actual, religious motives; without, in other words, treating them as partners rather than quasi-official arms of state.

The tension is well expressed by the historian, Frank Prochaska, with whom we started this chapter.

> A degree of tension between the state and voluntary sectors is inevitable. The essence of charity, like the essence of voluntarism generally, is its independence and autonomy – it is the antithesis of collective or statutory authority. Government provision depends on compulsory taxation; it is not altruistic but materialist in conception. It is largely about furthering equality. Charitable provision, on the other hand, cannot be extorted by force; its proponents have usually been driven by individualist rather than egalitarian motives. Historically, the work of charity has been an expression of a liberal polity, at odds with an egalitarianism in which rights take precedence over duties. Distinctions between charity and government action are thus deeply rooted, not least in thinking about their respective roles and boundaries. The perennial question remains: where should the balance lie between the "right" to welfare and the "virtue" of charity?[48]

twenty-first century Britain will see a lot more of God in the public square.

Politics, however, is about questions and tensions, and just because there are and will remain questions about how the two partners in this dance of civil society are to move together, that does not change the fact that every indication is that "a greater degree of partnership between the state and charities now seems inevitable".[49] For this reason alone, twenty-first century Britain will see a lot more of God in the public square.

chapter 3 - references

1   Frank Prochaska, *Christianity and Social Service in Modern Britain: The Disinherited Spirit* (CUP, 2006), p. 6

2   Frank Prochaska, *Christianity*, p. 6

3   Frank Prochaska, *Christianity*, p. 41

4   Framk Prochaska, *Christianity*, p. 44

5   Frank Prochaska, *Christianity*, p. 65

6   Kathleen Heasman, *Evangelicals in Action: An Appraisal of their Social Work in the Victorian Era* (Geoffery Bliss, 1962), p. 14

7   Frank Prochaska, *Christianity*, p. 24

8   See, for example, Roy Hattersley, *John Wesley: A Brand for the Burning* (Little Brown, 2002), p. 402

9   AJP Taylor, *English History 1914-1945* (Oxford: OUP, 1965), p. 455

10 Nicholas Timmins, *The Five Giants: A Biography of the Welfare State* (HarperCollins, 1995; rev. 2001), p. 6

11 See Niall Fergusson, *The Cash Nexus* (Allen Lane, 2001)

12 Frank Prochaska, *Christianity*, p. 149

13 Frank Prochaska, *Christianity*, p. 154

14 Frank Prochaska, *Christianity*, p. 154

15 William Beveridge, *Voluntary Action: A Report of the Methods of Social Advance* (London, 1948)

16 Frank Prochaska, *Christianity*, p. 153

17 Frank Prochaska, *Schools of Citizenship: Charity and Civic Value* (London: Civitas, 2002), pp. 41-48

18 Frank Prochaska, *Christianity*, p. 162

19 Frank Prochaska, *Christianity*, p. 46

20 Social capital is commonly defined as "networks, together with shared norms, values and understandings which facilitate cooperation within or among groups." It is closely related to the idea of civil society.

21 Charles Pattie, Patrick Seyd and Paul Whiteley, *Citizenship in Britain: Values Participation and Democracy* (CUP, 2004), p. 189

22 Charles Pattie, Patrick Seyd and Paul Whiteley, *Citizenship*, p. 268

23 Charles Pattie, Patrick Seyd and Paul Whiteley, *Citizenship*, p. 267

24 Paola Grenier and Karen Wright, *Social capital in Britain: an update and critique of Hall's analysis*, LSE, Centre of Civil Society, International Working Paper 14, 2003

25 Charles Pattie, Patrick Seyd and Paul Whiteley, *Citizenship*, p. 57-107

26 See www.nwda.co.uk

27 Northwest Regional Development Agency, *Faith in England's Northwest: Economic Impact Assessment* (2005)

28 East of England Faiths' Council & University of Cambridge, *Faith in the East of England (2005)*

continued…

chapter 3 - references

29 See, for example, R Furbey, A Dinham, R Farnell, D Finneron and G Wilkinson, *Faith as social capital: Connecting or dividing?* (Joseph Rowntree Foundation, 2006); B Cairns, M Harris and R Hutchison, *Faithful regeneration: The role and contribution of local parishes in local communities in the Diocese of Birmingham* (Birmingham: Centre of Voluntary Action Research, Aston Business School, 2005); Yorkshire Churches, *Angels and advocates: Church social action in Yorkshire and the Humber*, (Leeds: The Regional Commission for Yorkshire and the Humber, 2002); J Flint and A Kearns, *The role of Church of Scotland congregations in developing social capital in Scottish Communities: Enabling and cohesive or irrelevant and divisive?* (Glasgow: ESRC Centre for Neighbourhood Research, Centre for Neighbourhood Research Paper No. 16, 2004)

30 Quoted in *Faithful Cities: A call for celebration, vision and justice* (Church House Publishing, Methodist Publishing House, 2006), para. 8.5

31 2003 Home Office Citizenship Survey: *People, Families and Communities* (Home Office Research Study 289, 2003)

32 Church House Publishing, Methodist Publishing House, *Faithful Cities,* para. 1.20

33 Charles Pattie, Patrick Seyd and Paul Whiteley, *Citizenship*, p. 276

34 Rowan Williams, Hansard, 19 May 2006, Col. 501

35 Northwest Regional Development Agency, *Faith in England's Northwest,* p. 4

36 East of England Faiths' Council & University of Cambridge, *Faith in the East of England*, Executive Summary, p. 2

37 Church House Publishing, Methodist Publishing House, *Faithful Cities*, para. 1.22

38 Rowan Williams, Hansard, 19 May 2006, Col. 503

39 *Faith in England's Northwest: Economic Impact Assessment*, p. 3

40 Church House Publishing, Methodist Publishing House, *Faithful Cities*, ch. 8 for more details

41 Rowan Williams, Hansard, 19 May 2006, Col. 503

42 Rowan Williams, Hansard, 19 May 2006, Col. 503

43 See R Furbey et al, *Faith as social capital* for more details

44 Frank Prochaska, *Citizenship*, p. 47-48

45 R Farnell, R Furbey, SS al Haqq Hills, M Macey and G Smith, *"Faith" in Urban Regeneration? Engaging Faith Communities in Urban Regeneration* (Bristol: The Policy Press, 2003)

46 R Furbey et al, *Faith as social capital*, ch. 8

47 From personal communication

48 Frank Prochaska, *Citizenship*, p. 45

49 Frank Prochaska, *Citizenship*, p. 47

the pursuit of happiness

"It's time we admitted that there's more to life than money, and it's time we focused not just on GDP, but on GWB - General Well-Being."

So spoke Conservative leader, David Cameron, at the Google Zeitgeist Europe conference in May 2006.

"It's about the beauty of our surroundings," he went on, "the quality of our culture … above all [it's about] the strength of our relationships." In other words, it's not (just) the economy, stupid.

Cameron's speech was reported as a major shift for his party, but the new road on which he was placing them was already becoming rather well trodden. Numerous books, papers and articles over the preceding years had discussed, analysed and attempted to find answers to one of the most important trends of our time: the decoupling of wealth and happiness.[1]

health, wealth and…?

The facts are well established. The British, like most Westerners, are richer than ever before. GDP per capita has risen almost constantly over the last 35 years, all but doubling between 1971 and 2004. Over this period, real household disposable income per head (the amount of money a household has available to spend or save) has increased even further, reaching nearly 2.5 times its 1971 level by 2003.[2]

We earn more than ever before, so we spend more than ever before. The total volume of domestic spending on goods and services reached 2.5 times its 1971 level by 2003, allowing for inflation. The greatest spending increases were for non-essential items, with people spending proportionally less on food, housing, water and fuel, and proportionally more on communication, holidays, recreation and culture. The British are not so much a nation of shopkeepers now as a nation of shoppers.

Accordingly, we own more than ever before: 99 per cent of UK homes have a TV and the average household has around 2.5,[3] 89 per cent have a video recorder, 50 per cent a DVD player, 84 per cent a compact disk player, 58 per cent a home computer and 48 per cent satellite, cable, or digital TV. In addition 96 per cent of homes have a fridge/freezer, 89 per cent a microwave oven, 57 per cent a tumble drier and 31 per cent a dishwasher. With respect to communication, 99 per cent of people have access to a telephone at home, 76 per cent to a mobile phone, and 48 per cent to the Internet. Out on the drive, 74 per cent of households have a car or van and 29 per cent have more than one. Most people in Britain live in a material paradise that would have left their grandparents speechless.

And we live longer and healthier lives in which we may enjoy the fruits of our labour. Life expectancy is ten years greater now for men and women than it was at the end of the Second World War.[4] Over the same period, infant mortality has fallen from 40 deaths per 1,000 births to under 5.

This is all genuine and inspiring progress. And yet ... all the evidence points to the fact that we are no happier than we were, say, 30 years ago, and some studies even suggest we are less happy. As Tony Blair said (of his generation) in 1995, "We enjoy a thousand material advantages over any previous generation, and yet we suffer a depth of insecurity and spiritual doubt they never knew."

Measuring a nation's well-being (or happiness or life satisfaction – the terms are often used interchangeably) is far from straightforward. One way of doing so is by looking at its opposite: personal psychological ill health at an individual level, or crime levels at a corporate level, although both of these must be treated with caution – approaches to prescribing drugs and recording crime have changed over the years. The fact, however, that the levels of obesity, alcohol and drug abuse, depression, sexually-transmitted infections, recorded crime, and the prison population have risen notably over recent decades does not suggest a population at ease with itself.

A better idea of people's happiness can be gained from what people themselves say about themselves in life satisfaction surveys.[5] In the early 1970s approximately a third of British people said they were "very satisfied" with life. By the late 1990s that proportion was unchanged. Referring to these findings, one academic paper notes laconically, "life satisfaction has run approximately flat in Great Britain. In a period of increasing material prosperity ... these results may surprise some observers."[6]

The UK is not alone. Other European countries have been similarly static. Despite a six-fold increase in income per head since 1950, the Japanese have recorded no increase in happiness.[7] In the US, reported levels of well-being have actually declined over the last 30 years.[8] Wherever one goes in the "developed" world, the evidence points to a decoupling of wealth and happiness. In the words of the economist and Labour peer, Richard Layard:

People in the West have got no happier in the last 50 years. They have become much richer, they work much less, they have longer holidays, they travel more, they live longer, and they are healthier. But they are no happier.[9]

It is important to emphasise that this does *not* mean there is *no* relationship between wealth and well-being. Figures show that richer countries tend to be happier than poorer ones, richer individuals tend to be happier than poorer ones in the same society, and the richer a society gets the happier it is. But in each of these cases the correlation exists *only up to a point*. Once a certain level has been reached, there is at best a very weak and at worst no correlation between wealth and happiness. After a certain point money does not make either nations or individuals any happier. In the US, for example, there is no reported difference in happiness between those on $20,000 per annum and those on $80,000. Similarly, nations such as Japan and Germany are no happier than Mexico or Indonesia, despite having considerably higher levels of GDP per capita.

how to be happy

This trend came as something of a shock. It didn't mean that it wasn't "the economy, stupid", in Bill Clinton's famous words, just that it wasn't *only* the economy. But if it wasn't only the economy, what was it? What does make us happy and, just as important, what can we do about it?

Addressing the first question is complex enough. A number of factors such as age, gender, looks, IQ and education have negligible or no impact on personal well-being. Others like one's genetic inheritance or health do, although not as much as one might intuitively think.[10]

Overall, studies suggest that six factors are significantly correlated to well-being: (in no particular order) money, work, state of governance, levels of interpersonal trust and community participation, family upbringing and relationships, and religiosity.

Money, as we have seen, is correlated to happiness, but only up to a point.

Studies show that the relationship between income and life satisfaction is both positive and statistically significant … but [that] the size of the positive effect of income is small compared to other factors such as marriage, divorce and unemployment.[11]

The second factor, work, is an important factor in two different ways. Unemployment is particularly destructive, with its loss of earnings, loss of self-esteem, lower social status, and reduced personal and social opportunities.[12] Conversely, and obviously, employment is linked to life satisfaction, although low levels of job satisfaction can sever this link. The more one experiences "personal control, variety, income, job security, skill use, and physical security" in one's job, the higher the level of job satisfaction tends to be, and the higher the consequent level of life satisfaction.

Thirdly, there is a state of governance. Factors such as stability, accountability, rule of law, absence of corruption and a greater sense of control over one's civic destiny are all positively linked to well-being. An analysis of the relationship between life satisfaction and democracy in Switzerland found that those who lived in cantons with more referenda and higher levels of direct democracy were happier than those who did not.[13] On a larger scale, it is common for those people living in countries, like Belarus, which exercise severe restrictions on freedom of speech, assembly and religion, to be among the most miserable in the world.

The fourth factor, the level of interpersonal trust and community participation, is one of the most important contributors to life satisfaction. Touching on the theme of the last chapter, evidence suggests that higher levels of trust within a community are directly linked to higher levels of happiness. "Preliminary research into the effects of levels of trust on life satisfaction shows that those who believe it is wrong to cheat on their taxes and those who believe people can generally be trusted are, on average, more satisfied with their lives."[14] Directly linked to this is a strong correlation between social engagement and life satisfaction. Perhaps not surprisingly, those who are very active in the community are more satisfied than those who never attend local groups.

Fifth, but most importantly, is the role of family upbringing and relationships. Family break-up has a very significant effect on personal happiness. If a child's parents split up, they are approximately twice as likely to become depressed, irrespective of age. According to the Labour peer, Richard Layard:

> if by 16 you are living with only one of your biological parents, you are more likely to suffer from multiple disadvantages, compared with other children. You are 70% more likely to have a criminal conviction by the age of 15; you are twice as likely to leave a school with no diploma; you are twice as likely to have a child in your teens; you are 50% more likely to be doing nothing by the age of 20. You are no better off if your mother remarries or if your grandmother moves in. As adults, people from single-parent families are more likely to die young and to get divorced themselves.[15]

The pattern continues into adulthood. Marriage is consistently shown to be the most important single factor within life satisfaction. Married people tend to be happier than those who never married or those who have divorced or separated or been widowed, a fact that holds across cultures and even when income and age are taken into account. Accordingly, divorce, separation or the death of one's spouse is more harmful than almost anything else.

Last, but by no means least, comes the God factor. Study after study records the importance of religiosity in its various forms. Thus, Richard Layard says:

One of the most robust findings of happiness research is that people who believe in God are happier.[16]

And the Prime Minister's Strategy Unit:

Religious people report higher levels of life satisfaction. Research, mostly into Christianity, has found a correlation between life satisfaction measures and religious certainty, strength of one's relationship with the divine, prayer experiences and devotional and participatory aspects of religiosity. Both the effect of religious belief *per se* and the social benefits provided by participation in religious activities have independent effects upon life satisfaction.[17]

> *One of the most robust findings of happiness research is that people who believe in God are happier.*

And the Australian economist, Clive Hamilton:

A sense of meaning and purpose is the single attitude most strongly associated with life satisfaction … religious commitment and participation consistently appear as significant contributors to life satisfaction … spiritual striving contributes more to well-being than any other type of goal, including the goals of intimacy, power and symbolic immortality.[18]

Hamilton goes on to refine this conclusion:

Research affirms that higher forms of spirituality … a search for meaning, for unity, for connectedness, for transcendence … contribute more to contentment than the rituals of church attendance and daily prayer – extrinsic manifestations of religion that may reflect nothing more than a desire for social acceptance, the internalisation of parental expectations, or an insurance policy against the possibility of an afterlife.

If, as the research indicates, it is these six factors – money, work, state of governance, levels of interpersonal trust and community participation, family upbringing and relationships, and religiosity – that make us happy, what makes us unhappy will be reasonably clear: the opposite.

That said, there is one factor that erodes our happiness that is not so obvious and is worth mentioning. Richard Layard talks about how exposure to advertising, and to violence and sex through media is correlated to life dissatisfaction. Not only can television reduce our social life and community involvement (a fact emphasised by Robert Putnam in *Bowling Alone*) but it exposes us to the world, especially in its more extreme forms, in such a way as to breed anxiety and, very often, a coarsened and brutalised outlook. Advertising places people on a "hedonic treadmill", which either fosters insecurity ("Life has enough embarrassments without your mobile phone being one of them") or promises happiness/freedom/sexual magnetism/etc. from your next purchase. Similarly, "people who watch more TV believe there is more crime in real life and more adultery than there really is … [becoming] desensitised to these activities and more willing to contemplate them for themselves."[19] The problem, Layard emphasises, is not television *per se* – there were no measurable increases in violence when TV was first introduced to 1950s' America – but its content.

Not surprisingly, the effect on children can be particularly serious. According to an overview of the relevant research published in the *Lancet* a few years ago:

> From a public-health perspective, there is evidence that violent imagery has short-term effects on arousal, thoughts, and emotions, increasing the likelihood of aggressive or fearful behaviour … Longterm outcomes for children viewing media violence are more controversial … nevertheless, a small but significant association persists in the research, with an effect size that has a substantial public-health effect.[20]

moving onto God's territory

This analysis of the factors linked with well-being, both positively and negatively, brings God back into the public square, although not in the way that one might at first think.

The obvious link between well-being and religiosity is also the least relevant. No one seriously thinks it is within any government's right to promote religious belief, no matter how closely correlated with well-being it is.

The more subtle and more important link has two strands to it, one general and one specific. The general strand is that religious thinking has long been concerned with well-being in a way that political thinking is now attempting to become. Religious groups have long preached (and sometimes even practised) value systems that have fostered well-being and acted as a counterbalance to the human inclinations towards greed and materialism that are so dominant in our overwhelmingly and overwhelming consumerist culture.

This is a point constantly made by those who have written on the emergence of well-being in the public square, irrespective of their own religious (non-) beliefs. Clive Hamilton writes:

> In the world of market relationships the inner worlds of feeling and spirituality were banished from the conscious mind and trivialised to the point where religious affiliation or expression of religious sense attracted derision. In popular culture, spiritual urges and religious convictions are disparaged, and a series of superficial arguments is advanced to prove the irrelevance and futility of religion – it causes more wars than it solves, it's a crutch for weak people, and so on. All this reflects a deeper transformation, the alienation of self from the seminal urge for meaning and the flight to the triviality of material consumption and frivolous gratification. In the end, religion is seen as "uncool", something that says much more about modern marketing culture than about the relevance of religious striving to the human condition. The argument here is not that well-being should or can be advanced through the promotion of religious belief or spiritual endeavour; it is that a society that scorns intrinsic religiousness and trivialises the pursuit of meaning discards thousands of years of insight and can only suffer for it.[21]

The argument here is not that well-being should or can be advanced through the promotion of religious belief or spiritual endeavour; it is that a society that scorns intrinsic religiousness and trivialises the pursuit of meaning discards thousands of years of insight and can only suffer for it.

Richard Reeves, writing for the think tank, the New Economics Foundation, makes the same point more directly:

> Given the orthodoxy of the grow-earn-spend philosophy, the case for the church and other religious agencies to act as counter-cultures has never been stronger.[22]

The second strand moves from the general point that religious value systems provide an important counterbalance to those held captive by consumerism, to the specific one that many of the factors that are most positively correlated with well-being are significant features of the major religions.

Thus, the lifelong, faithful, monogamous marriage that contributes so much to personal and social well-being has long been central to major religious traditions. The focus on the family as the best environment in which to raise children, now recognised as one of the two or three biggest contributors to human well-being, is, again, central to most religious traditions. Campaigns about broadcasting standards, so often associated with religious groups, and derided by the mainstream, might, after all, have something profound to contribute to our communal life. Trust and community participation, closely correlated with personal, social and economic flourishing, are, as we noted in the previous chapter, central features of faith groups today. Even health is affected. "In a recent systematic review of scientific literature that uncovered 100 studies of this relationship [between religious beliefs and practices, and well-being and mental health], 79 per cent reported a significant positive association." [23]

All this means not so much that religion is coming back into the public square, as the fact that the public square itself is shifting, orienting itself around the question of well-being, and in so doing, moving into territory that religions have inhabited for many centuries. The public square is coming back to God, rather than the other way round.

To be sure, religious engagement in the question of well-being far exceeds anything that the political community should or will be concerned with. The *Compendium of the Social Doctrine of the [Catholic] Church* describes how:

> the common good of society is not an end in itself [but] has value only in reference to attaining the ultimate ends of the person and the universal common good of the whole creation ... a purely historical and materialistic vision would end up transforming the common good into a simple *socio-economic well-being*, without any transcendental good, that is, without its most intimate reason for existing. [24]

The object of politics and the goal of human flourishing, as understood in Christianity, are not the same thing. Yet, the slow reorientation of the former indicates that they will share more common ground in the future than has recently been the case.

If all this is true, we are still left with the second "enormous" question mentioned above: what can we do about it? Or rather, what *should* we do about it? Religiosity may be positively correlated with well-being, but that doesn't mean government should "compel the worship of a higher being", as *The Economist*'s review of Richard Layard's book on happiness pointed out. [25]

The question is unlikely to find an easy, popular or widespread answer, people's responses depending on their view of the right and proper objectives of government. David Cameron, for example, in the speech to Google, rejected regulation, claiming that "rules, processes and systems imposed from above will ... undermin[e] the personal relationships that we should be aiming to strengthen," favouring exhortation and example instead. Those closer to the other end of the political spectrum would, of course, disagree.

There is no reason to suppose that religious thinkers, across or within particular traditions, will agree on the solutions any more than politicians do. But that is neither here nor there. The fact remains that if politics is to regain and retain public interest it will need to venture into well-being territory, as David Cameron, Tony Blair and others have argued. And, in doing so, it will find itself sharing the public square with the religions that some had imagined were gone for good.

chapter 4 - references

1   See, for example, Richard Layard, "Happiness: Has social science a clue?" Lionel Robbins Memorial Lectures, London School of Economics, 2002/03; Richard Layard, *Happiness: Lessons from the new Science* (Allen Lane, 2005); Clive Hamilton, *Growth Fetish* (Pluto Books, 2003); Andrew Oswald and David Blanchflower, "Well-being over time in Britain and the USA" *in Journal of Public Economics*, 2004; Nick Donovan and David Halpern, "Life Satisfaction: The state of knowledge and implications for government", Prime Minister's Strategy Unit, 2002.

2   C Summerfield & B Gill (eds.), *Social Trends 35* (Office for National Statistics, 2005)

3   The figure of 2.5 TVs per household is from www.ofcom.org.uk The others in this paragraph from the Office for National Statistics' *General Household Survey 2003* (www.statistics.gov.uk)

4   See *A Century of Change: Trends in UK Statistics since 1900*, House of Commons research paper 99/111

5   These too have obvious problems, such as being susceptible to moods and circumstances, but are conducted and analysed so as to address such problems. See Richard Layard, *Happiness*, for details.

6   Andrew Oswald and David Blanchflower, "Well-being"

7   Richard Layard, "Happiness: Has social science a clue?"

8   Andrew Oswald and David Blanchflower, "Well-being"

9   Richard Layard, "Happiness: Has social science a clue?"

10 Health is a complex factor. Self-reported health is strongly correlated to life satisfaction but more objective measures of health are not. People become habituated to some forms of ill health but not to others. Mental health is strongly correlated with low levels of well-being.

11 Nick Donovan and David Halpern, "Life Satisfaction," para. 39-40

12 These factors are slightly mitigated if you "live in a region with a high unemployment rate; have family members who are also unemployed; or you have been repeatedly unemployed in the recent past." Nick Donovan and David Halpern, "Life Satisfaction," para. 8

13 Quoted in Nick Donovan and David Halpern, "Life Satisfaction," para. 15

14 Quoted in Nick Donovan and David Halpern, "Life Satisfaction," para. 73

15 Richard Layard, *Happiness*, p. 61

16 Richard Layard, *Happiness*, p. 72

17 Quoted in Nick Donovan and David Halpern, "Life Satisfaction," para. 74

18 Clive Hamilton, *Fetish*, ch. 2

19 Richard Layard, *Happiness*, p. 85-90

20 K Browne and C Hamilton-Giachritsis, "The influence of violent media on children and adolescents: a public-health approach" in the *Lancet*, 365: 702–10 (2005)

21 Clive Hamilton, *Fetish*, p. 53

22 Richard Reeves, *The Politics of Happiness* (New Economics Foundation, 2003)

23 H Koenig and HJ Cohen (eds.), *The Link between Religion and Health: Psychoneuroimmunology and the Faith Factor* (OUP, 2002)

24 Pontifical Council for Justice and Peace, *Compendium of the Social Doctrine of the Church*, sect. 174

25 "Can't buy it," in *The Economist*, 13 January 2005

the politics of identity

January 2005 was an odd month. Just as Christianity was slipping back into the shadows after its annual Christmas airing, it found itself back on the front pages. The BBC had decided to broadcast a stage version of the controversial show, *Jerry Springer – The Opera*, making a few people rather unhappy.

The whole affair was deeply shocking, not so much because the show was blasphemous or contained hundreds of expletives, but because so many Christians actually bothered to do something about it. Fifty thousand people complained, more than for any other show in the BBC's history. One group applied for a judicial review, claiming the show had breached the BBC's charter and broken the Human Rights' Act. Another published the home phone numbers of BBC executives and latterly persuaded the cancer charity, Maggie's Centres, to turn down a £3,000 donation from the show.

All this was made more newsworthy because the previous month had seen hundreds of Sikhs demonstrate outside Birmingham's Repertory Theatre about a play, *Behzti*, which depicted sex abuse and murder in a Sikh temple. The demonstration turned violent. Five police officers were hurt and several protesters were arrested. The play closed. Not since *The Satanic Verses* had the debate between artistic licence and cultural and religious sensitivity been more acute.

As if all this were not enough, the publication of cartoons of Mohammed in Danish and other European newspapers a year later heralded further demonstrations and violence. Although no UK paper published the cartoons,[1] a significant number of Muslims protested in London. Initial demonstrations were aggressive and insensitive, with protestors carrying placards saying things like "butcher those who mock Islam" and "Europe you will pay, your 9/11 is on the way", but subsequent ones were more peaceful.

A few months later, the London-based Asia House, due to host an exhibition of one of India's most renowned artists, Maqbool Fida Husain, acquiesced to the threats and intimidation of a Hindu campaign that claimed that the artwork was insulting and offensive.

All this has outraged liberal opinion, proving, as if proof were needed, that religion is an authoritarian, backward-looking relic of humanity's infancy, whose invariably toxic contributions to public debate were sufficient grounds to ban it from the public square.

Despite the ammunition that such affairs offer polemicists, however, the real issue is more subtle and related to more than the feelings of a few religious minorities. Religion is only the most visible aspect of a debate that is in fact about identity.

Jonathan Sacks explains this well in his book, *The Dignity of Difference*, when discussing Francis Fukuyama's vision of liberal capitalist democracies as being "the end of history":

> What this overlooked … is that homo sapiens is not only, or even primarily, a maximising animal, choosing rationally between options. We are uniquely a meaning-asking animal. Our most fundamental questions are Who am I? and To which narrative do I belong? The great hope of the liberal imagination, that politics could be superseded with economics, replacing public good with private choice, was bound to fail because economics as such offers no answer to the big questions of "Who?" and "Why?". Religion does, and that is its power in the contemporary world. The politics of ideology may have died, but it has been replaced not by "the end of history" but by the politics of identity.[2]

Humans are "committed, moral, believing animals."[3] Any clash of civilisations is essentially a clash of narratives, a clash of different ways of seeing, engaging and living in the world. Religions are commonly at the forefront of such conflicts because they have some of the world's oldest, most fully formed and deeply loved narratives.

It is, nevertheless, a mistake to see this solely as a religious issue, a mistake fed by the most pervasive myth of our age, that liberal humanism, and the states for which it provides the intellectual foundations, is neutral rather than itself a particular narrative. No matter how much we might like to pretend otherwise, "we… do not have at our disposal a universal, indubitable foundation of knowledge by which to judge our own and others' beliefs and stories neutrally, objectively and definitively."[4]

The fact that this issue is one of human identity rather than religious sensitivity can be seen in the growing interest in citizenship, an interest that long predates 7/7 or even 9/11. The collapse of four historic pillars of Britishness – union, empire, monarchy and Protestantism – that had been so central to national identity for so long, combined with the large-scale migration that the UK has enjoyed over the last 15 years, has urgently posed the question asked by Yasmin Alibhai-Brown's eponymous book: *Who do we think we are?*

It is a question with legion implications. As Gordon Brown said in his 2004 British Council lecture:

> I believe that just about every central question about our national future – from the constitution to our role in Europe, from citizenship to the challenges of multiculturalism - even the question of how and why we deliver public services in the manner we do - can only be fully answered if we are clear about what we value about being British and what gives us purpose and direction as a country.[5]

The story that we choose to tell about ourselves shapes us economically, politically, socially and culturally. That story has historically emphasised freedom and tolerance, but those qualities, unless counterbalanced by more substantive ideas of collective identity, end up dissolving the ties that bind. As nothing significant has filled the gap left by the decline of our traditional identity, the British are unclear what it is that makes them British.

The result has repercussions in virtually every sphere. Those closely linked areas of migration, community integration and national security are only the most newsworthy. Equally important is the one that David Goodhart raised in his article for *Prospect* magazine entitled "Discomfort of Strangers". Quoting David Willets, Goodhart wrote:

> The basis on which you can extract large sums of money in tax and pay it out in benefits is that most people think the recipients are people like themselves, facing difficulties that they themselves could face. If values become more diverse, if lifestyles become more differentiated, then it becomes more difficult to sustain the legitimacy of a universal risk-pooling welfare state.[6]

Goodhart went on to say:

> Too often the language of liberal universalism that dominates public debate ignores the real affinities of place and people. These affinities are not obstacles to be overcome on the road to the good society; they are one of its foundation stones.

It is these "real affinities of place and people" that are set only to grow in importance in the twenty-first century, and not just in the UK. Holland, long the archetypal liberal society, has experienced several years of painful introspection, as high levels of immigration and several high profile murders have forced a re-evaluation of national values, resulting (so far) in the introduction of citizenship tests for immigrants, a sizeable increase in visa fees, and the imprisonment and deportation of failed asylum seekers. The new politics of identity raises some awkward questions and has led politicians down some difficult and surprising roads.

religious animals

All this has proved something of a double shock to enlightened opinion. Firstly, the belief that a liberal society of equality, non-discrimination and largely unrestricted personal freedom was what the world had been waiting for has been proved wrong. There are people who see things differently, many of whom cannot simply be dismissed as ignorant or uneducated.

Secondly, and more worryingly, religion is a major ingredient in this new mix. People's religious beliefs are not only not quietly private, they are not even quietly public. Not only is God not dead, but he seems strong enough to wield a megaphone and a placard.

Shocking as this is, there is little sign of such issues going away. Indeed, every indication is that the politics of identity, of different narratives, of clashing and possibly even incommensurable value systems, is moving centre stage.

All the trends that feed this development are set to grow in importance: economic globalisation, large-scale migration, EU enlargement, cheaper and easier communication, cheaper and easier travel. Accordingly, more and more commentators are talking of the shift, popularised through Philip Bobbit's book, *The Shield of Achilles,* from the nation state to the market state, in which, "the function of government … is to clear a space for individuals or groups to do their own negotiating, to secure the best deal or the best value for money in pursuing what they want."[7]

If the politics of identity is here to stay, does that mean religiously-motivated political engagement is too? The answer is almost certainly yes.

This may surprise those who have become accustomed to judging the health of religion through annual Church of England attendance figures, but the fact remains that, as observed in the introduction, religious belief and adherence is in good health around the world. This alone suggests that religion will play *some* part in future public debates about British identity, unless the nation desires to seal itself off from the globalising trends that now shape the world. Even if British-born citizens are less overtly religious, foreign-born citizens are unlikely to be.

In any case, declining church attendance does not mean secularism or atheism. This point has been made, albeit brutally, by Professor John Gray:

> Of all the myths spawned by the Enlightenment, the idea that we live in a secular age is the most absurd. Throughout much of the world, religion is thriving with undiminished vitality. Where believers are in the minority, as they are in Britain today, traditional faiths have been replaced by liberal humanism, which is established as the unthinking creed of conventional people. Yet liberal

humanism is itself obviously a religion – a shoddy derivative of Christian faith notably more irrational than the original article, and in recent times more harmful. If this is not recognised, it is because religion has been repressed from consciousness in the way that sexuality was repressed in Victorian times. Now as then, the result is not that the need disappears, but rather that it returns in bizarre and perverse forms. Secular societies may imagine they are post-religious, but actually they are ruled by repressed religion.[8]

Whether or not one agrees that liberal humanism is "a shoddy derivative of Christian faith", Gray's basic point that suppressing religiosity does not make it disappear is undeniable. The history of the Soviet empire provides ample evidence of this. Closer to home, social research in the UK shows that the level of belief in all kinds of bizarre and fantastical phenomena, from mediums to memes, has *increased* over recent years. MORI's 2003 British Public Opinion report recorded that:

In January 1950, only 10% of the public told Gallup they believed in ghosts, and just 2% thought they had seen one. By 1998 we found that 40% now say they believe in ghosts, and 15% that they have "personal experience" of ghosts; 6%, indeed, said they had based a decision on their belief in ghosts. Similarly, in 1951 only 7% of the public said they believed in foretelling the future by cards, and 6% by stars; in 1998, 18% of the public said they believed in fortune telling or tarot, and 38% in astrology…

"This," the report concludes, "leads to what some would describe as a more credulous society."[9]

> *Secular societies may imagine they are post-religious, but actually they are ruled by repressed religion.*

Oddly enough, it is often religion's most hostile critics who are offering support for the idea that mankind is an innately religious animal. Lewis Wolpert, Daniel Dennett and Robin Dunbar, none of whom is a noted friend of organised religion, have each written suggesting that untrue and harmful as they may be, religious beliefs seem to be woven into the fabric of being human. Thus, Robin Dunbar concludes his book, *The Human Story*, by saying:

As remarkable as our achievements in the arts and sciences may be, it is hard to escape the conclusion that religion is the one phenomenon in which we humans really are different in some qualitative sense from our ape cousins … We should not, in our haste, overlook the important role religion has played in human affairs, helping to bond communities and so enabling them to meet the challenges that the planet has thrown at them. Even today, its contribution to human psychological wellbeing is probably sufficient to raise serious questions about whether the human race could do without it.[10]

Of course, the fact that humans are in some way innately religious does not mean that religiosity will necessarily be part of the public square. Some religious traditions consciously shun any public presence, and it is hard to see how our stubborn belief in astrology will become a public phenomenon in any meaningful sense of the phrase. Nevertheless, if the twenty-first century is to be marked by the politics of identity, it is equally hard to see how those well-formed, deeply-rooted identities of the major world religions will not also mark it.

a policy of inclusion

For some people, albeit a minority, this does not constitute a reason to admit religion into the public square. They argue that whether or not we are innately religious, admitting religious groups into the public square gives them, and more pertinently, gives their ever-present extremist wings, the oxygen of publicity. Evicting them and safeguarding the public square's (supposedly neutral) secularity is the only way of drawing the poison of fanaticism (and, hopefully, too of religion).

In actual fact, there is mounting evidence to suggest that it is precisely this approach that feeds fanaticism, and that, on the contrary, it is by including religious groups in public debate that society can draw whatever poison they might otherwise deploy. Writing about faith schools in *Public Policy Research*, Jodie Reed says:

> Some argue that faith schools have the capacity to speak to the heritage of pupils and thereby can provide a powerful tool for instilling moderate interpretations and preventing radicalisation. There may be something in this: drawing on 265 international case studies, one report found that only 9 percent of extremists had an Islamic primary or secondary background. The remaining 91 percent went to secular schools.[11]

A comparative study of "Muslims and the state in Britain and France," published in the same issue of *Public Policy Research* offers similar conclusions.[12] The authors argue that "Britain's church-state model has been an important institutional and ideological resource for Muslim activists and has opened up opportunities for Muslim political mobilisation," in two ways in particular.

Firstly, "it encourages Muslims to press the state to accommodate their religious practices in the same way that the state accommodates other religions," and secondly, "it enables Muslim leaders to make the argument for a public, political role for religion." The presence of an albeit gentle and inclusive religious tradition in the public square has helped protect and stabilise society.

By contrast, because French politics is an arena of sometimes aggressive *laïcité*, "it has been impossible for Muslims to put on the policy agenda such things as support for separate Islamic schools or state aid for Muslim social service organisations." This, in turn, has "inhibit[ed] the successful integration of French Muslims and exacerbate[d] social tensions between ethnic North Africans and *Français de souche*."

The authors conclude:

> If arguments in favour of this kind of laïcité continue to prevail, it will be difficult to convince Muslims that the French state genuinely grants them "equal opportunity and respect". Such a strict reading of laïcité is disastrous for Muslim integration and it is not hard to understand why some Muslims express hostility to a state that has been unwilling to allow such unproblematic demands for religious practice as the wearing of the hijâb. From a Muslim standpoint, such a policy is not neutral toward religion, but instead hostile, and explicitly preferences a secular over a religious worldview. This breeds hostility among Muslims toward French culture and society which propels already disaffected and segregated communities further from the political mainstream and into the arms of radical Islamists.

This conclusion touches on a number of themes mentioned in this book, not least the questions of social cohesion and state neutrality, but for our purposes here it is sufficient to note that the authors argue that it is public recognition and not suppression of religious beliefs, motivations and identities that contributes to social harmony.

It should not need saying (but, again, regrettably will) that treating religious groups as valid participants within the identity debates to which modern politics is gravitating does not mean failing to scrutinise or criticise them. Indeed, it means the very opposite. If religious groups wish to participate in this area of the public square, they must be willing to defend themselves without recourse to sectarian or inscrutable reasons. They must be self-critical and willing to utilise (if also challenge) public reason. That is the price of admission. It is precisely inclusion of this nature that "is likely to qualify any extreme positions. If you have to argue your case and negotiate in the public realm, you are obliged to work with the standards and assumptions of people who don't share your convictions; and this can (challengingly) extend the conversation on both sides."[13]

The alternative, as Richard Chartres, Bishop of London, has pointed out, is not appealing:

> If you exile religious communities to the margins, then they will start to speak words of fire among consenting adults, and the threat to public order and the public arena, I think, will grow and grow.[14]

chapter 5 - references

1   Mystifyingly that well-worn cliché, "Freedom means nothing if not the freedom to offend" was largely absent from newspaper editorials at the time. For an overview of the UK press response see http://news.bbc.co.uk/1/hi/uk/4677474.stm which concludes: "such restraint is unusual in the British media these days."

2   Jonathan Sacks, *Dignity,* p. 40-41

3   See Christian Smith, *Moral, believing animals: Human personhood and culture* (OUP, 2003) for a definition and exploration of this idea

4   Christian Smith, *Moral,* p. 89

5   http://www.hm-treasury.gov.uk/newsroom_and_speeches/press/2004/press_63_04.cfm

6   David Goodhart, "Discomfort of Strangers", *Prospect*, February 2003

7   Rowan Williams, The Dimbleby Lecture, 2002

8   John Gray, "Sex, atheism and piano legs", in *Heresies: Against Progress and other illusions* (Granta, 2004), pp. 41-48

9   MORI, British Public Opinion 2003

10 Robin Dunbar, *The Human Story* (Faber and Faber, 2004), pp. 197-199

11 Jodie Reed, "Religion and schools in England", in *PPR* 12.4. The study she quotes can be found in Marc Sageman *Understanding Terror Networks* (University of Pennsylvania Press, 2004)

12 J Christopher Soper and Joel S Fetzer, "Muslims and the state in Britain and France," in *PPR* 12.4

13 Rowan Williams, The Nicholas Hinton Lecture, given at the AGM of the National Council for Voluntary Organisations, 17 November 2004

14 "The Godless Continent", *Analysis*, Radio 4, Broadcast 21 April 2005

how to "do God"

This report has essentially been a rubble-clearing exercise, an attempt to clear away some of the objections to letting God into the public square and to create a space for public theology by arguing why religious engagement in public debates should and, in all probability, will increase in twenty-first century Britain.

It has tried to practise what it preached (in chapter 1) by using publicly accessible reasoning to make its case rather than specifically theological arguments, except in chapter 2 where the question in hand was theological.

It has also been a self-consciously positive effort, making the case for "doing God" by examining the problems, prospects and merits of that path, rather than by carving chunks out of alternative ideologies and attempting to show how inadequate they are.

This point is important because, as argued in chapter 1, religiously-inspired participation in the public square can be divisive, with opposing parties speaking past, or worse, spitting insults at one another. The best way of preventing this is to adopt a tone of respect and arguments that are primarily constructive rather than destructive.

That said, it is worth noting one final trend that constitutes another reason why religious engagement in the public square may grow in twenty-first century Britain. This is the challenge, or more accurately the challenges, facing the liberal humanism that has so long provided the intellectual foundations for the public square.

Liberal humanism is, like every other complex ideology, difficult to define. Broadly speaking, however, it is premised on a combination of the beliefs (i) that human beings are qualitatively different from other animals and thus merit particular respect; (ii) that they possess free will and are, therefore, moral agents; (iii) that they value freedom as an ultimate good; (iv) that the state can be neutral concerning its citizens' different conceptions of the good life; (v) that there are "basic ideas" about human freedom and equality on which all reasonable people will agree and on which an accepted conception of political justice can be based; (vi) and that a better future both can and will be built. By no means everyone who calls themselves a liberal humanist will countersign all these statements, but between them they capture the essence of the ideology.

The problem is that over recent decades every one of them has come under sustained attack. Studies of primates and other animals have raised serious questions about human exceptionalism, with individuals like Peter Singer and Richard Ryder arguing that humanism is unacceptably "speciesist" and that human rights should be extended to all creatures capable of suffering pain and distress. Along similar lines, a number of scientists question the notion of free will, arguing that the human concept of choice is illusory and that humans are not, in fact, moral agents.

The liberal deification of personal freedom is being placed under severe strain in many Western nations, as fears about terrorism, crime, immigration and social cohesion are orienting governments towards ever more anti-libertarian measures, in the belief that electorates ultimately value security over liberty.

> *The liberal deification of personal freedom is being placed under severe strain in many Western nations.*

The foundational liberal idea that the state can be neutral is increasingly doubted, as is the idea that human reason alone can locate common conceptions of the good or that there are "basic ideas" about human freedom and equality which can be worked up into a universally accepted conception of political justice. Whether this is due to the argument that human rationality is not universal but always historically placed, or that human values are ultimately plural and incommensurable, or that our modern ideas of universal values are little more than a kind of post-colonial imperialism, this particular pillar of liberal humanism looks decidedly shaky.

Finally, the optimism about human nature, "that human nature will triumph, that human nature is a basically good thing,"[1] that has fuelled liberal humanism since its birth looks unconvincing (to put it mildly) as the human race looks back over a century of genocides and ahead to a century in which our treatment of non-human creation promises to deform the planet as never before.

None of these charges is proven, let alone a deal clincher. Moreover, a number are just as challenging to some religious traditions, not least Christianity, as they are to liberal humanism (not surprisingly given the shared lineage of those two belief systems). Nevertheless, the fact remains that by weakening the intellectual foundations of the creed that has been the self-evident basis of the public square in recent times, such arguments cannot but open up that square to other creeds, among them religious ones.

avenues of engagement

If this conclusion and those of other chapters are warranted, we are still left with the rather bigger question, how should we "do God?" This question is beyond the remit and scope of this report, but the issues discussed above gesture towards four avenues of engagement.

Firstly, given the inclination of both the government and the main opposition party to partner with voluntary organisations, foremost among them religious ones, for the provision of public services, it seems that, in this respect at least, God is here to stay. This, however, begs numerous specific questions.

Reports on the role of faith groups within civil society consistently draw attention to the particular difficulties such groups have in working with ill-informed and sometimes aggressively secular local authorities with short-term funding regimes and burdensome levels of bureaucracy.[2] If government wishes to partner with voluntary organisations, particularly religiously-inspired ones in the future, such issues need addressing. How should the dance between government, local authorities and religiously-motivated voluntary groups be choreographed? What is the appropriate level and form of regulation, of accountability, of mutual comprehension, of religious ethos, of metrics to measure success? How should the need to control funds and ensure success be balanced against the drag of endless form-filling and the uncertainty of short-term funding horizons? Such questions already occupy the public authorities, and need to be addressed equally seriously by public theologians.

If these specific questions constitute one avenue of engagement, a second but more fundamental one is the bigger question as to whether we should be doing this at all. To ask this is not to cast doubt on those arguments outlined above, but rather to recognise that there is real debate *within* religious groups about whether this "New Establishment" is theologically justifiable.[3] How clear is the line between social action and evangelism? Can churches legitimately do both and, if so, how can they balance them? In the words of Pope Benedict's first encyclical letter:

> Charity … cannot be used as a means of engaging in what is nowadays considered proselytism. Love is free; it is not practised as a way of achieving other ends. But this does not mean that charitable activity must somehow leave God and Christ aside.[4]

The Church is not simply a cheap, efficient, well-meaning arm of the state, conveniently compliant and docile as long as the funding rolls in. For the most part, those Christian groups involved in fostering civil society know this. Yet, "as charitable agencies become increasingly accountable to government, they are prone to forfeit their role as critics of government policy. [As] a charitable official put it nearly ten years ago: 'no one is rude to his rich uncle'."[5]

Different theologians respond to this dilemma in different ways and this is only to be expected.[6] Political theology is, like politics, an arena for debate. The fact is that however the presence of God makes itself felt in the public square, this debate is likely to be of foundational importance. What good is it, after all, for a church to gain a whole world of funding and forfeit its soul in the process?

A third avenue of engagement is that relating to public reason. This report has argued that religious groups that wish to participate in the public square must be willing to argue their case at the bar of public reason, framing their arguments in such a way as to include rather than alienate those who do not share their primary motivations. This, as mentioned briefly in chapter 1, is little more than an outworking of the doctrine of accommodation.

But I have also argued that Christians, and indeed people of other religions, should not accept public reason at face value and should, accordingly, be willing to question the presuppositions that underpin it. What is "reasonable" is, as already noted, far from obvious and those that claim otherwise need to be able to defend themselves.

This, in effect, amounts to a call to all participants in the public square to "show your workings". Too often there is an implicit two-tier system at work in public debate. In this system certain opinions, such as the need to maximise individual choice or to release information whenever possible, are treated as axiomatic – indisputable, shared by all sane people and too obvious to need justification. Other opinions, usually but not always religious ones, are seen as differing from the norm and thus in need of particular defence. Thus, the argument for retail deregulation is supposedly clinched by the idea that people should have the choice to shop where and when they like – when was the last time you heard anyone ask why people should have the choice? – whereas arguments against it demand a more complex exploration of family and community life, the survival of local retail ecology, and the protection of workers' rights.

This is not to question the need for choice (or freedom, or equality, or efficiency, or tolerance, or any other of our society's supposed axioms) but to suggest that none of these values is, in fact, axiomatic and that these building blocks of our (current system of) public reason need exposing and defending.

One story might illustrate this. In 1964, the *New Scientist* assembled over a hundred experts to explore the "likely developments of the next twenty years". In the process of their discussions, the group anticipated something very similar to the Internet.[7]

An immediate situation will develop with private ownership of computers of limited capabilities which also serve as remote terminals to communicate with centrally located computers. The entire content of the large central files will be readily retrievable at a moment's notice.

This impressive prediction was followed by the less than inspiring forecast of which fields would be most affected.

The consequences will be truly profound in many diverse fields, such for example as agronomy, jurisprudence and medicine.

The Cabinet Office's Performance and Innovation Unit noted these predictions in a report and went on to remark:

Had contributors taken account of the fact that what most people are really interested in … is social communication, market interactions (buying and selling) and sex, then they would not have been surprised to learn that the main uses of the Internet would be social e-mail, e-commerce and pornography.

The point of this story is to remind us that a myriad of invisible beliefs, many of which are not religious in the usual sense of the word, underpin and shape our thinking. In this instance, the *New Scientist's* experts unthinkingly believed that human nature progressed alongside technology and that the development of (something like) the Internet would, in turn, reshape human nature and concerns. This belief is, as John Gray likes to point out, little different from a religious one. Yet somehow, in spite of the fact that the doctrine of human progress is an article of faith just like the resurrection or the divine inspiration of the Koran (an article that is, arguably, rather harder to believe), it is rarely noticed, let alone defended.

The fact of public reason, therefore, places two demands on those religious thinkers who wish to participate in the public square. They should be willing to accommodate their language and reasoning to what is currently acknowledged as the norm in public discourse. But they should also be willing to challenge that norm, questioning axioms, confronting arguments and asking all parties, irrespective of their public identities, to justify their faith-based positions.

This third avenue of engagement leads us to a fourth and final one that, in turn, brings us back to where we started. If we all need to show our workings, we need to be less jittery when other people's workings seem foreign to us. Given the current nature of the public square this, in effect, means we should not react with bewilderment when a public figure does "do God". We should be less scared of public figures citing religious texts in mainstream contexts. We should be more willing to treat other value systems as coherent, reasonable and even valuable rather than as primitive or grotesque mutations of the liberal humanism to which every sane person adheres. And, assuming we wish to invite faith groups to provide welfare services, we need to recognise openly the particular beliefs that motivate them.

To be sure, all this comes with a *quid pro quo*. A politician who mentions Jesus Christ, St Paul, Thomas Aquinas or Mohammed in public must be prepared to explain why that figure has any bearing on the issue in hand. One who cites a religious text must be willing to defend its relevance and validity. Most importantly, any public figure who introduces God into debate must be sure he is not doing so for personal or divisive reasons. To allude to God simply in order to imply he favours me over you is to make a mockery of the idea of God as he has been understood in the Judaeo-Christian tradition.

With such caveats in place and a public that is sufficiently vigilant to ensure that God does not slip from being a political figure into being a party-political one, there is no reason against and plenty of reasons for "doing God" in twenty-first century Britain. Even if the deity is unlikely to be such a prominent resident of Downing Street after Tony Blair's departure, at least for the foreseeable future, he seems to have a bright if not uncontroversial future in the public square.

chapter 6 - references

1   Roy Hattersley, in "A Human Politics", *Analysis*, Radio 4, Broadcast 16 March 2006

2   See, for example, *Faith in Urban Regeneration? Faithful Cities*, ch. 7

3   Luke Bretherton, "A New Establishment? Theological Politics and the Emerging Shape of Church-State Relations" in *Political Theology* 7.3

4   Pope Benedict XVI, *Deus Caritas Est*, sect. 31(c)

5   Frank Prochaska, *Christianity*, p. 167

6   In his essay on the New Establishment Luke Bretherton looks at the different views of four major contemporary Christian thinkers: Stanley Hauerwas, John Paul II, and Oliver and Joan Lockwood O'Donovan.

7   "The World in 1984", *New Scientist* 1964, quoted in Performance and Innovation Unit, *The Future and how to think about it*, 2000 (http://www.strategy.gov.uk/downloads/work_areas/strategic_futures/Future.pdf